D1621664

CHILD
DRAMA
IN
ACTION

REMOVED FROM
E.S. EUGENE SHEDDEN FARLEY LIBRARY
FARLEY LIBRARY
WILKES UNIVERSITY
COLLECTION

WILKES COLLEGE   WILKES-BARRE, PA.

CHILD
DRAMA
IN
ACTION
A PRACTICAL
MANUAL
FOR
TEACHERS

BILLI TYAS

DRAMA BOOK SPECIALISTS/PUBLISHERS
150 West 52nd St., N. Y., N. Y., 10019
(212) JU 2-1475

GAGE

PN3171
T9

Designed by Gene Aliman
Illustrated by Garry Hamilton

COPYRIGHT © GAGE EDUCATIONAL PUBLISHING LIMITED, 1971.
PRINTED AND BOUND IN CANADA
All rights reserved — no part of this book may be reproduced
in any form without permission in writing from the publisher.

Reproducing passages from this book by mimeographing or by
photographic, electrostatic or mechanical means without the
written permission of the publisher is an infringement of copyright law.

Affectionately dedicated to
The General

171304

FOREWORD

In this book the author is facing up to a very difficult task. Despite our understanding of the process of children's creative play, there has been full recognition of the average teacher's difficulty over a practical approach.

"Child Drama is a voyage of self-discovery. The child is the captain, the adult is merely the navigator." This point is made very clearly and indicates that we must not impose too much but should rather suggest ideas about action, ask children also for their ideas, and then leave proper time for action by the children to take place without our showing them how to do it. This is where things often go wrong. Teachers often talk too much and cannot therefore leave enough time for the children to "do." The child as captain indicates the need in each one of us to discover slowly, not only what we can do but who we really are. This is a deep need in human nature. "Particularly in this computer age, it is essential that the child be educated to be aware of his creative power and helped to realize this power." In an age when more and more equipment is being provided for education, we must safeguard the active, dynamic side of the personality, which can only be fully realized through opportunities for personal play.

It is pleasing to see that each lesson states what is the *purpose*, or main emphasis, of its work. Sometimes people try Child Drama—however bravely—because of a fashion or because they think it ought to be done, but are not quite sure why they are doing it. We must not be too rigid, but there must be a meaning to what we do.

A final point made is that exercises suggested must not on any account be slavishly followed; they are only intended to start things off.

I hope this book by Billi Tyas will give many teachers the courage at least to start, though they will soon find that they have to be flexible. I would say to them, don't try to do it all yourselves. Trust your children enough to discuss progress with them frequently, and you may find that you can build wisdom together.

Peter Slade

Birmingham,
England
November, 1969

PREFACE

The author of this book uses the term Child Drama because it puts the emphasis where it belongs, on the child. The lesson situations and the vocabulary used are designed specifically to suit children in the primary grades, but the units can also be used with older children who have had little or no previous experience of this type of structured creative activity.

The book is intended to be used as a manual by teachers actually engaged in doing dramatic work with their classes; it can also be used as a text in teacher colleges, faculties of education, and departments of drama where the use of child drama is taught, either within the language arts program or as a separate subject. Its combination of theory and practice makes *Child Drama in Action* a valuable aid in an area in which idealism has often been offered to teachers more freely than practical guidance.

Though brief, the author's Introduction is extremely important. It states clearly and concisely the basic theory and goals of child drama ("What is Child Drama?"), and indicates its potency as a means of self-development for the child ("The Value of Child Drama in Education"). The third section ("Your Work in Child Drama") gives valuable advice, and particular attention should be paid to the breakdown on page *xv* of the underlying structure of each lesson.

The pictures at the beginning of over half the units are provided to help suggest to the teacher a mood and some imaginative possibilities; they are specifically designed for the teacher's enjoyment, not for the children.

The lesson plans themselves are given in complete detail. At the beginning of each is a statement of the theme, a note of a particular aspect of the activity to be emphasized, and a list of the materials that will be required. Then follow, in effect, two texts. The one, printed in color, indicates what the teacher should do and the things she or he should watch for—and also wait for. The other, printed in black, is the actual script, which provides a pattern for the setting of the atmosphere and the development of the situation. This script is printed as the author has spoken it in her classes, and it has the life and vividness of speech. It is not intended that the teacher must read the script word for word; she can do so if she wishes, but it is preferable for the teacher to study the unit carefully beforehand and then to develop the situation in her own words, reacting to the creative responses of her own children but keeping to the basic structure of the unit. She will thus use the two texts rather as a conductor uses the score of a familiar symphony—not as a crutch, but as a reminder of who should be doing what and of what should be going to happen next. The typographic separation of the two texts, and the indication (□) in the script of places to pause for the children's participation, should make it easy for the teacher to concentrate on the children and to refer to the book only as necessary.

The teacher must always be free to respond to the inventiveness of the moment. She must also give the children the freedom to contract or expand the treatment of a given situation. Governed by the children's response, she may sometimes do well to suggest a completely different twist to a theme—or even to break off and switch to another activity. The children themselves can often suggest alternative lines of approach that can be fruitful and rewarding. If interest in a situation is sufficiently intense, she may want to come back to the same situation in a later class—not to repeat what has been done but perhaps to enlarge it, or to tackle the same theme in a different way.

Some of the units in the book will almost certainly spread themselves over two classes. In fact, it must be emphasized that there is nothing especially significant in the fact that there are 22 units in the book rather than 24, 25, or even 30. There should be enough material here for one class a week through the school year, but the important thing is not the quantity of material covered; what matters is the quality of the children's experiences.

CONTENTS

INTRODUCTION

What Is Child Drama?

Child Drama is NOT Children's Theatre! Theatre, in all its forms, reveals drama as a mirror held up to man which reflects his nature in society or in an environment; it is a cultured convention of a civilized people. The artists of the theatre spend many years training their talents in the disciplines of its art form and require an audience to witness the images they create.

On the other hand, real life reveals drama when the individual man steps into the mirror, participates in the experience created by his environment, and discovers truths about himself, his society, and his world. Such drama has no rigid art form; it does not require a script. The settings, the plots, and the emotional content vary with the personalities and are as mottled as men. This drama does not demand a skilled talent for a person to take part in it; everyone possesses the natural gift to participate, even the most primitive man. *Dran*—the ancient Greek word from which the word *drama* is derived—means "to do"!

Doing has always been the first tool man has instinctively used to equip himself for his survival in life. In ancient Greece, which is the root of our western civilization, doing was the first tool used in the education of man for the living of life. To these educators it seemed that the spirit of man was composed of three elements: instinct, feeling, and thinking; the ideal goal was to find the proportion and harmony of these three, so that through this knowledge of self man could become in tune with his life.

In the element of instinct it is natural for the child to do—to play; children play with things, then play being things. By using this unlearned tendency— this instinct—we can lead the child to experience the dramas of life and, through his participation in channelled dramatic play, the way is opened for him to discover his world and his own self; he is also enabled to experiment, for himself, with the

proportions and harmony essential for living his life. While play has always been the inalienable right of childhood, it was not until the nineteen-thirties that Peter Slade, in England, from his own detailed observations of children at their natural play, isolated dramatic play as an entity in itself and developed its use in education, defining it as Child Drama.

Child Drama is channelled creative play; the child struggles toward achieving a goal he has invented for himself from the leader's suggestions. With this guidance Child Drama nourishes his two basic quests for fulfilment: "Am I useful?" (the use of self for society) and "Am I worthwhile?" (the use of self in society). The realized use of self *for* society requires the child to discover and refine his talents so that they can be of value. The realized use of self *in* society requires the child to be aware of his instinct, feeling, and thinking ability and to develop their controlled usage in harmonious proportions. All work in Child Drama contributes to satisfying these two needs for the child's development, and it is based on his natural forms of play, projected play and personal play. Through doing projected play, the "I" experiences being useful; through doing personal play, the "I" experiences being worthwhile.

Projected play is when a child is creating a tangible object as a product of his intellect, imagination, and talent to achieve a goal. When he has finished with his creation, he can then, if he chooses, divorce himself from the object and leave it as a monument of his concentration at that moment in time. As a simple example: a child decides he wants to make a snowman. He creates a snowman. When the child has made his snowman, if he wishes, he can run off and leave it. It may no longer interest him; the snowman has served its purpose for the child. He knows "I can make a snowman"; he saw his accomplished work. The "I" has experienced usefulness, and the snowman exists as the monument of his energies. The opportunity to practise projected play in a Child Drama lesson is given to the children when they create caves, houses, mountains, coaches, castles, ships, or crowns and swords out of the available material. In the everyday school classroom one can see daily the evidence of a child's projected play in his tangible creations from his other studies, especially his art and written work. The use of projected play from Child Drama can be of great value to the child if it is introduced into his lessons on art, science, and mathematics.

Personal play occurs when the child is creating his goal out of his imagination, intelligence, and talent with his "self," and he may then involve his creation in a situation. In this form of play he cannot divorce himself from his finished creation, he is one with it. What is left of this experience is a memory, a vivid picture in his mind of his concentration at that moment in time. As an example: the child creates a king. His king regally greets his queen and courtiers in the castle. From the response of the others in the drama, he knows he moved like a king should, he behaved like a king should; indeed, at that time, he was the king of that castle. The "I" has experienced being worthwhile; the child has realized within himself the harmonious proportions he needed to create that king of that castle.

The components of personal play are running play and role playing. Running play is the child learning the use of his body for a purpose, and through the use of this knowledge he can explore his personal use of space, sound, and rhythm. As an example: a child wants to learn to skip. First he gains the knowledge of how to use his feet, arms, and body to produce a skip; and then through the act of skipping he can test his personal use of space, sound, and rhythm. Role playing is purposeful action in a given situation. This form of play demands subjecting oneself to the experience of sharing with others the inflow and outflow of one's emotions and thoughts in response to people or objects. Two examples are: a child trying to persuade mother that he is sick and can't go to school; and a child entering a dark room by himself to go to bed. The opportunity to practise personal play in a Child Drama lesson is given to the children when: (a) in running play they are various people and things: clowns, horses, trees, princesses, or children standing in their own shoes and doing every kind of movement and all forms of the dance; and (b) in dramatic play when as children themselves, or as statues, elves, flames, or soldiers, they partici-

pate in a situation together.

Role playing is a prevalent practice in our society, and it is the basis of much of children's play. It is also, when the opportunity is provided, a potent force in education. Its use in language, history, and geography classes allows children to expand their present experience and to become aware of the reality of what they are studying. The last five lessons of this book offer examples of how this may be done, being based on themes from history, myth, and folklore.

The child can be led to evolve himself into a happy, whole person who can find his place to stand in his society through the absorption of his experiences in the personal and projected play of Child Drama.

The Value of Child Drama in Education

In a child's development, the results of his participation in Child Drama cannot be scored in ratings, but its merit is manifested by the extended use the child makes of his creative power in all his activities.

His creative power originates in the brain. Among its many functions, the brain has the ability to think in pictures (to make images) and is the monitor of the emotions as the centre of the nervous system. Both these dynamic functions of the brain, although they may operate independently, can respond together to a stimulus of the senses. Medical and psychological research now has evidence that the nervous system, in its response to a stimulus of the senses, cannot distinguish between an actual or a simulated experience if it is vividly imagined in detail in the laboratory of the mind.

These recent findings endorse a practice which many advanced educators have followed in the past. A vividly imagined environment or situation can be recreated in detail with the children, in such a way that they can become deeply involved, under controlled conditions in the classroom. Thus we can make children aware of life without causing them to be burnt in its flames. This teaching method is the foundation for the development of the inner child through Child Drama; it challenges the child to discover his individual self and his individual potentiality. Because each child's response is a valid expression for him, the child understands he is only in competition with himself and thus gains a sense of security. His feeling of fulfilment comes when he learns how to use his mind and talents toward successfully achieving a goal. He also becomes aware of how to motivate and discipline himself and his emotions, both in his own behavior and in his relations with others.

We are not assessing the child's external behavior as to how well he relates to the adult standards expected of him, but we do perceive how capable he is of being able to relax and use his real self in *his* society. We are helping him to develop his "self" and find his place to stand. This cannot be accomplished in ten or twenty lessons; but each experience of his true nature, which he encounters during a Child Drama class, gives him the confidence on which he may build his own development throughout life.

Child Drama is a voyage of self discovery. The child is the captain, the adult is merely the navigator.

The measure of the success of the leader's work as the navigator is in direct proportion to the measure of happiness *each* child experiences. The child's happiness is based on the opportunity given him to experiment with the use of his creative power (imagination and emotion), and the result gains him praise. With the leader's approval, even though it may be a silent understanding because he is not criticized, the child knows achievement. Then he can dare to destroy his own creation, if he feels it was not to the limit of his capabilities at that time, and select a greater goal more worthy of his self-expression.

Particularly in this computer age, it is essential that the child be educated to be aware of his creative power and helped to realize this power. We can offer the child this important opportunity through Child Drama by re-creating with him, and for him, varied situations and different environments within the walls of the classroom. The child gains out of these experiences an improved ability to listen, to think creatively, to concentrate, to express his ideas freely and coherently, and to accept his responsibility to himself and to others.

Your Work in Child Drama

When you read over the following units, you will notice that there is an established format used in each one. Creative work cannot be set in a definite mould because, throughout your creative work together, it is hoped that you and the children will contribute further dimensions to the shared experiences of a unit; however, the format does give you a spine for your work during the class. The unit is structured in an easily related pattern for the child, and its gradual procedure is designed to provide stepping stones of achievement required for the child's development. To aid his development, your main purpose, in every class, is to stimulate the child's imagination and enlarge the store of his experiences. The special emphasis in each unit is intended to heighten each child's awareness, and in addition it offers you a specific aim for that particular session. The extent of the children's use of the knowledge derived from what they have experienced in a unit enables you to assess the results of your work with them.

The following is a breakdown of the structure which is used in the units:

1. To stimulate the children's imagination at the beginning of the unit, the entire class is given something very simple to do. They move about, creating and absorbing the impressions you suggest to them. In "The Forest" and "The Fair" units they become aware of trees, leaves, birds, clowns, or ponies.

2. To stimulate their intellect and imagination there is a class discussion. The children give their individual impressions and absorb other childrens' impressions of the event.

3. This is practice in running play. As a class, with everyone working at the same time, the children are some of the creatures they have discovered and discussed, such as clowns, ponies, or princesses, and they experience these creations in action.

4. At this point in the unit, for practice in role playing, the children in small groups individually experiment with using their creative powers in a given situation, and all the groups work at the same time.

5. The children practise personal and projected play through their dramatic play together. In this last part of the unit, first each child helps conceive and construct a required habitat, then he is his individual creation and together these creations become involved in a drama.

By the time the child comes to the drama, these structural phases of the unit have enabled him to experiment and to assess for himself the elements needed for his creation. If you make sure that the child knows "who he is" and "what he is doing" in the drama, he can achieve—he can do it!

As the leader, in your approach to all your work with the children, you must believe in Child Drama and make it possible for them to believe in their creations through your attitude. You are given two keys: (a) always to guide the children in their work with assurance, and (b) to keep your imagination keen and flexible at all times.

Some Do's and Don'ts

I TO BE READY:

1. DO remember the scene is set for Child Drama in the land of the imagination, and absorption can only take place in this land. The child needs inspiration from a sympathetic leader to adventure into this land.
2. DO give the opportunity for everyone to do everything. No stars!
3. DO give a purpose to every action a child is asked to carry out: "I think the fire is out" or "The circus is over, we come back home."
4. DON'T tax the concentration of a child at any one thing. He cannot be absorbed in "doing" for very long.
5. DO ascertain the child understands each time "who he is" and "what he is doing" in all forms of his play.
6. DON'T judge a child's work, you may only assess it. The individual is only in competition with himself; he alone has the privilege to compare and criticize his effort.
7. DO stress "you are." It is a positive approach to the child. He can do it. Don't use, "you are going to be" or "be anything"; the child will always be at a loss to know how he should express himself.
8. DO listen to children and their ideas. Discussion periods are important for the child to relate and expand his knowledge and experiences, pleasant and unpleasant.
9. DO let the children use such available materials as chairs, tables, rulers, waste-baskets, levels of any kind and rostrum blocks—if you are fortunate enough to have them—in their play.

10. DON'T tell children to "speak up." Rather encourage them to share their voice with us. As a child gains his confidence he will make himself heard.
11. DO ask the children to "share" their good work with the class, not "show" it to them.
12. DO use questions to challenge the child to think for himself. Statements are likely to stunt mental gymnastics.
13. DON'T forget—there are no wrong answers. Each child's response may be valid for him.
14. DO expect some noise and chaos during class. Be calm, this same melee is a natural breeding ground for the child where he learns to create—to bring order out of his confusion.
15. DO allow the children plenty of time to experiment with their creative powers from each of your suggestions during a class. Insincerity and superficial experiences develop when the children are rushed at their work; wait for that last child to become involved in the "doing."
16. DON'T give up!

II TO BE STEADY—in your purpose of Child Drama:

1. If the children ask "Are we going to put on a play?" the simple answer is: "Another day, today we are going to have some fun doing (x)" and begin work immediately. Another day doesn't usually come as the children discover the joy in doing their own dramas.
2. The mothers and staff want to see the children "do a play." DON'T weaken! Remember, theatre is another art form in itself—this is drama, the story of the doing of life. They are children, not performers, and any audience is apt to make a circus of their efforts. A casual visitor to the class, or an occasional arena style "happening," should acquaint the most insistent adults with your work.
3. There is a stage evident in your working area. Shut the curtains and forget it.
4. The hall is too big. You will lose the children's attention. Using any means available, section off a smaller working area.
5. The class is too large—16 is the ideal number. Divide your time and divide the class. It is especially important in the initial lessons.
6. You have to take the whole class at once—the

entire forty children! Never mind, do the best you can. Follow the pattern of the unit until the doing of the drama, then divide the class into groups of eight at most and have several versions of the drama in turns.

7. You have a classroom to use. If possible, push back the desks to give you a decent working area. These same desks can be a valuable asset to the children in creating their habitats for their dramas.

8. The children are bored and inattentive. Think fast and give them something very active to do. It will revive all your energies.

9. Johnny Jones, or maybe several boys, insist on showing off and disturbing the class. Remember, children learn by their experiences. Be kind and be polite, but always keep control of your class. Move yourself to stand close to the boys, maybe even put your hand on a shoulder, and go on with your work. If your presence does not deter them, by your magic, turn them into rocks or lamp-posts, which requires that they remain still until you feel they are interested and would like to re-join the class.

10. First-lesson jitters. The teacher and children are nervous, both have a fear of the unknown. Introduce yourselves to each other as friends would, and then get to work at once; when you become involved, you can all relax.

III TO GO:

1. DO experience Child Drama as an adventure for you and the children. The child is the captain, you are the navigator, and the units are the charts for the course. Be resourceful and daring. The charts are only intended as guidelines for the voyage; follow and expand them in your own way.

Enjoy it.

ONE

Theme:

THE FOREST

Emphasis:

Developing self-control in response to a drumbeat

Materials: Drum.
Record.
  SUGGESTED: *In a Monastery Garden*, Ketelbey.
  ALTERNATE: *The Trout Quintet*, Schubert.

At the beginning of the class ask the children to come close around you and sit comfortably on the floor. When you have their attention, begin:
We are going to have a wonderful adventure, right here in this room today. Each one of you, shut your eyes. □ Instead of this being an ordinary room, by your magic see if you can make it full of trees. □ In fact, because you see there are so many trees, it becomes a forest. Isn't it a lovely woods? □ Now open your eyes; you can, by magic, still believe for yourself that the room is full of trees. It is such a beautiful day, let's all go for a walk in our woods.
Put on a record. (Smooth-flowing, pastoral music. Suggested: *In a Monastery Garden*, Ketelbey.)
Now get up and walk anywhere you want and explore your woods. What kind of trees do you see?
During their walk in the woods, when you suggest each new thought, give the children sufficient time for them to be able to create it in their imagination, to really see and experience it for themselves. During this exercise do not expect any spoken answers from the children; it is important only that you interest them in the doing of the activity.
Is the sun shining through the leaves of the trees?

Can you see the blue sky above the trees? What was that song you just heard? Was it a bird's song? Where is he? □ Are there any animals in the woods? What kind? □ Look for them. □ Where are they? □ There's a stream ahead, let's jump over it. □ Good, you made it; no wet feet! Are there any leaves on the ground? Pretty colored ones? Let's pick up some really beautiful ones to bring back with us. □ The sun is going down; we had better head for home. Do bring your leaves with you, and since it's getting late we had all better hurry. Come back home, over here.
Indicate the place.
Come quickly before it gets dark. □ There, we are all home safe and sound.
Fade out music.
Sit on the floor and rest.
The children arrive back and sit on the floor near you, bringing with them their imaginary leaves. Ask questions about the leaves—as to their shape, size, color, or what kind of tree they are from—as a starting point for a discussion with the children. Encourage the children to talk, and do take the time to listen. If time and the children's interest permit, ask them additional questions based on the lesson narrative, such as: "What color bird?" "What kind of animals?" This gives the children a chance to express their ideas freely. Try to give each child a chance to answer at least one question. If, after a

short while, you are getting only simple answers, such as "red," "green," "high," "short," and you can sense the children's attention beginning to wane, go on to the next part of the lesson to recapture their interest.

Put all your beautiful leaves carefully down on the floor.

Produce a drum. The use of the drum not only teaches the child control of movement, but the starting and stopping of beats helps to give you control of the class.

What does a drum remind you of?

Accept their answers and, through questions relating to parades, lead the children to suggest "soldiers." From this suggestion, continue:

You are all soldiers, marching. Off you go, in a circle around the room. Now listen carefully. Because this is a very fine army, whenever there is a loud beat on the drum, on the very next beat, the soldiers stop marching and all stand still where they are. Let's try it. □

Beat a marching rhythm of 1,2,3,4, finishing with a loud beat and then the extra beat on which the children are to stop.

Good, but I heard one or two extra footsteps. Let's try it again, and let's see if this time we can *all* stop together. □ Careful not to lose your balance when you stop. This time we are all tall soldiers. □ And now little, short soldiers. □ And now you are fat soldiers □ and thin soldiers. □ This time you are any kind of soldier you like, and you are going to make a drum sound with your feet to the beat that I will clap. Be careful to listen and keep your feet beating in time—and sometimes the beats might stop!

Clap the beat instead of using the drum, stopping frequently.

Good. What a fine army you are! All you soldiers must be very tired; sit down where you are and have a rest.

On the drum make a light quick tapping sound.

What do you think your feet would be doing to make that sound?

You are seeking the response of jumping, skipping, hopping, or running.

Shall we all stand up again and see if we can hop to that drumbeat? □ skip to the drumbeat? □ and jump to the drumbeat? □ What animal would make the same sounds with his feet as he moved through the woods? □

From the association of skipping, hopping, jumping, the children will probably give the answers of rabbits, deer, or kangaroos. Use the children's ideas, and use the same light quick drumbeat to suggest:

You are all rabbits jumping through the woods. □

Now you are deer. □ And big kangaroos jumping along. □

On the drum, beat a slow, heavy sound.

What animal does this sound remind you of?

Lead the children to give the answer "bears." Remember there are no "wrong" answers, but if you don't get the answer you need for a take-off point at any time in the lesson, you can suggest: "Do you think it might be ......?" The child will usually agree with you and accept the idea as his own.

Bears? What color are they? □ What size? □ You are all big bears walking in the woods. □

Use the heavy slow beat on the drum.

See if you can be ferocious bears.

To this same beat, use any other animal, such as an elephant or hippopotamus, suggested by the children and have them experience the animal in action.

Good. What big heavy animals you are!

Repeat the same heavy slow sound on the drum.

Think what sort of people would make that same kind of sound with their feet. What would they be doing?

Accept the children's answers and lead them to suggest "giants" and to realize that the giants would be walking, not running, skipping, hopping, or jumping.

You are all big giants walking over the hills. □

Beat the same rhythm again.

Can you see over the tree-tops? □ Can you reach out and touch the mountain? □ Look at the big footprints you have made. □ Now stop and listen to this sound.

Produce a light slow beat, in a stealthy manner, on the drum. To elongate the beat, slide the drumstick across the drum.

What animal would make a sound like that as he moved along?

From the children's answers, select "a lion."

You are all lions creeping through the forest.

Begin the same drumbeat.

Stretch out your feet carefully, looking for the traps. □ Don't get caught. Good. Now think — what might a man be doing if he walked in the forest to that same sound?

Accept the answer of "hunting" and repeat the same sounds on the drum for the following.

You are all hunters. Carry your gun carefully: don't hold it up; point it toward the ground. □ Look around for the animals. □ Stop and listen for them. □ Now, take a partner, and the two of you hunt together. □ Be sure your partner keeps very quiet as you walk through the forest. □ I think the hunt is over now. Put your guns away. □ All come over here and sit down. □

Indicate a place near you.

I know a wonderful story we can do together about a hunt in the forest. We'll say there is a palace over there.

Indicate a location in the room where the palace is going to be set.

The palace is guarded by the king's soldiers and in it lives the king, the queen, a prince, and a princess, who are all fast asleep. In the morning they wake up and decide it is a lovely day for a holiday. They plan to make a picnic and go hunting in the woods over there.

Indicate the location of the woods.

With the soldiers to guard them, they march to the edge of the woods where all the animals live. It is a hot day and after their long walk, the king, the queen, the prince and the princess sit down and have their picnic.

The animals play around in the woods, then come to the edge of the woods to see the people from the palace. The king and queen fall asleep and the soldiers are relaxing. The prince and princess think it would be fun to enter the woods and hunt the animals by themselves. But the animals run and hide so that no one can shoot them. The king and queen wake up and call the prince and princess; the little hunters return to their parents; and with

the soldiers they all march home to the palace. All the people are happy; they have had a lovely day in the woods. The animals are happy; they run out of their hiding places and eat up the remains of the picnic lunch.

Let's divide into two groups and do that story.

Divide the children into two groups of roughly the same size. Indicate one group.

This group is the animals. Each one of you decide which animal you are. Run over to the woods and begin to make a house for yourselves out of the chairs or whatever you can find.

Indicate the other group.

In this group are the people who live in the palace. What people do we need for our story?

Give the children in this group the opportunity to decide among themselves which role each one is going to play. If they need help, guide them in their choices. For example, ask the children: "Who are the soldiers?" "Where do you stand?" "Perhaps one of you would like to be the drummer and play the drum for the soldiers to march to." Children like to help and be given responsibility for such things. Always take the attitude that they are capable of doing whatever you suggest to them.

To the children in the palace group, say:

You can make your palace out of these chairs or whatever else you can find?

Observe, and help the children of both groups in the construction of their "houses." Make sure that each child knows who he is in the drama. When their "houses" have been constructed, start the story.

Now we'll begin. Let's say it is night time when everyone is asleep except for the soldiers guarding the palace. They are on sentry duty, marching up and down in front of the big doors. □ In the morning the king and queen, prince and princess wake up. □ All the animals in the woods wake up and see the lovely morning and go in search of their breakfast. □

Narrate only as much of the story as is required to give the children the impetus to move the action along. Allow enough time to let them become involved with the story and to do it at their own speed, suiting it to their own actions and any dialogue they may use. After the children have played the drama, comment on their work. Always be truthful to them. If it has been a good class effort, they will know it and you can tell them so. Conversely, if the drama hasn't gone well, they will also know it, and you can say that it was a very good try but you wonder what went wrong. They will usually tell you! By the children's own recognition of their failure to achieve the goal together, each child is aware of the personal contribution required from him for the group's success in future dramas. If time permits, or if you carry this story over to a second lesson, allow the groups to exchange places if they wish, so that the "palace people" are the "animals" and vice versa. Although the children enjoy the repetition of the familiar, you may, if you feel they are ready for it, suggest the following addition to the story the next time they do the drama.

Would you like to add to our story this time? Let's say that, when the prince and princess are hunting in the woods, they become very tired and fall sound asleep under the trees. The king and queen wake up from their nap and call the children, but there is no answer. The king and queen go into the woods to search for the prince and princess, but they can't find them anywhere.

Because it is so quiet, the animals begin to re-appear and, when they see the king and queen haven't any guns, they lead them to the lost prince and princess. The king is so happy to find his children that he declares that this is a royal forest and there will be no hunting allowed here ever again.

The king, queen, prince and princess return to the palace with the soldiers. The animals eat the remains of the lunch for their feast, and they play happily ever after in the royal forest.

Begin the story in the same way as previously, and let the action proceed according to the children's own interpretation. At the end of the drama thank them for all their good work as a class.

TWO

Theme:

THE FAIR

Emphasis:

Developing freedom in movement and speech

Materials: Drum.
Records.
    SUGGESTED: "Victor Herbert Favorites,"
        from *Concert in the Park.*

Give a loud beat on the drum to gain the children's attention.

Let's see if you can walk to the drumbeat and stretch so tall that your fingertips touch the ceiling! □

Use a slow, steady beat for this action and also for each of the two following movements. End each section with a loud beat.

Good. Stop. Now we'll think you are so fat and round that you hop from one foot to the other as you walk along. □ And stop. That was great fun. Now your body is so light that you don't make a sound with your feet as you walk over here. □

Indicate a place near you.

Very good. I didn't hear one footstep. And now everybody sit down on the floor. □ How many of you have ever been to a fair? □ Did you go to the Exhibition (or use local name of the fair in your town) this year? □ It's the holidays again, and this afternoon we are all going to a fair. You each have plenty of money in your pockets, and off you go through the entrance gates.

Start the record. (A lively medley of gay tunes.

Suggested: "Victor Herbert Favorites," from *Concert in the Park.*)

See the big buildings, the fountains! A man is selling ice cream from a cart. Let's buy an ice cream cone. □ What kind did you choose? □ There are people everywhere; careful where you are going. Look at the funny hats some people are wearing. There's a man selling them over there. We must have one too. Try on some hats, and buy the one you like best. □ Oh, that's a lovely one! Now we are at the amusements. Just look at them all! See the Ferris wheel going around. Look, the seats are going high up into the air! Don't they stay up a long time? Scary, isn't it? Over there is the merry-go-round; it has brightly-painted horses to ride on. Over there is another ride. Let's buy a ticket for the ride you want to go on. □ Now have your ride. □ O-oh, we are shaky when we come off. Here we are at the Midway. There's a man guessing your weight. See if you can fool him. □ Did you? □ There are some more booths—a fish pond, a shooting gallery; and at this booth you can throw balls at the milk bottles. Let's see if you can knock the bottles down. □ You did! Now choose any prize you like. □

It's getting late; we had better start for home. Don't drop your prize. It's getting darker and darker. See, all the lights are coming on. Let's run back home here.

Indicate the place.

Run as fast as you can. Sit on the floor and rest as soon as you arrive back home. Wasn't that a wonderful day!

Fade out the music. A discussion with the children on their experiences at the fair follows. The prizes they have brought back with them are a good starting point. Finish the discussion with the children describing the kind of ball they threw at the milk bottles. This will lead into the next part of the lesson. The following is an example of the kind of discussion that might occur.

Mary, did you win a prize? □ What did you choose? □ Was your prize a big one, John? □ What is it? □ Who else has a prize? □ Peter, would you like to tell us about yours? □ Susan, will you show us your prize? □ Isn't that lovely! What do any of you other children think Susan has in her hand? □ Have they guessed? □ Then will you tell us what it is? □

Jean, what was the ride you chose to go on? □ What was it like? □ The ride you went on, Joey — how do you think it worked? □ Did anyone go on the Ferris wheel? □ What could you see when you were at the top? □ George, what part of the ride you were on did you like best?

How many chose a hat with a feather? □ Jane, can you tell us about the color and the kind of feather it was? □ What other kind of hat did anybody buy? □ John, tell us about yours. □ And you, Peter. □

Michael, when you threw the balls at the milk bottles, what sort of ball did you use? □

Did anyone use a different kind of ball? □ Mary, what kind was it? □

Now, we'll think that each of you has a medium-sized rubber ball like a tennis ball. Take the ball in your hand and, just as you are sitting there, spin it on the floor. □ Throw it up and catch it several times. □ Now bounce it a few times. □ Stand up, and to the drumbeat bounce the ball all around the room. □

Use a rather fast beat on the drum.

Bounce the ball on the ceiling. □ Throw the ball up against the wall and catch it on each drumbeat. □

For each throw and catch, give on the drum a slow beat of 1 and 2. Repeat the various suggested throws several times.

Throw them against the wall under your leg. □ Now over your shoulder. □ Between your legs. □ Don't forget to turn and catch the ball each time. Now throw them against the wall any way you want. □ Now throw the balls away. □

Choose a partner. □ One of you has a ball for the two of you to play with together. Listen to the beat of the drum and play catch with your partner. Try to throw and catch the ball on each drumbeat.

For the following actions, repeat the slow beat of 1 and 2. Also, vary the speed and loudness of this beat to make it suit the various kinds of balls that you suggest.

Throw and catch. Throw and catch. □ Good. Now let's try a heavy ball, still throwing and catching it on the beat. □ Now try a light beach ball. □ Have a snowball fight. Be sure to pack the snowballs well, and listen for the beat to throw them each time. □ That was a wonderful snowball fight.

Change partners. □ What are some other games that we play with a ball? □

One at a time, repeat the children's suggestions for ball games. They hit, kick, or throw the ball — as in tennis, ping-pong, football, volleyball, or whatever is suggested — on each drumbeat.

Clear all the balls away and let's place a line of chairs in the middle of the room. □

You will need only enough chairs for half the class. The chairs are placed all facing in the same direction. Stand in two lines on either side of the chairs. Each line faces the other. □ Do any of you know what jugglers are? □ What kind of balls do they use for their juggling? □ How many balls do they usually juggle at once? □

With a gesture, indicate the line of children who are facing the seats of the chairs.

The children in this line will be the orchestra, and they kneel down facing the front of the chairs; they can then use the seats of the chairs as drums. The children in the other line are the jugglers, and we'll say that each juggler has three balls to juggle to the rhythm that will be played by the orchestra.

Which one of you in the orchestra would like to be our leader this time and set the rhythm for us? □ Good. John, you will start a beat for us on your drum and the rest of us will listen; then the orchestra will join in with the same beat; and then the jugglers will begin to juggle the balls to the rhythm being played.

Ready. Begin, John, and we will listen carefully. □ Now the orchestra joins in, □ and the jugglers begin juggling the balls. □ Quite good. Could someone else in the orchestra think of another rhythm? All right, Mark; you start the beat this time.

Give two or three children a chance to have a turn at being the orchestra leader. Each child sets the beat of his choosing for the action. After a short while, reverse the groups and continue working with the children in the same way as before until their interest begins to wane.

Let's stay in our same groups, and we can make a merry-go-round together. The orchestra group who have just finished playing can move their chairs and make a circle over here.

Indicate the place.

Place the backs of the chairs together, with the seats facing into the centre; then stand inside the circle, each facing a chair. The other group are the children who are going to ride on the merry-go-round. You form a circle around the outside of the chairs. Each of you in the children's group, choose the kind of horse or other animal you would like to ride on. □ All set? This is going to be hard for us to do. All the riders face in this direction.

Indicate a counter-clockwise direction.

Get on your animal and be ready to move around when the orchestra starts. The orchestra will move slowly around in the opposite direction, this way.

Indicate a clockwise direction.

And they will beat the rhythm on the seats of the chairs as they go around. Peter, would you like to be our orchestra leader and start a rhythm for us? □ Good. Now, everyone join in and begin to move to that rhythm, and do your part to make our merry-go-round go round. □

After a few minutes say:

And stop. A very good try! Shall we do it again before we change places? All right, Jane, you think of another rhythm for us. □ And away we all go! □ That was a fine merry-go-round.

Each group quickly change places and we'll try it again. □ Jimmy, you haven't had a turn as the

orchestra leader. See if you can think of a faster rhythm this time. □ Good. We will all have to think harder when we move around to that rhythm, so that we don't miss the beat or lose our balance. Begin that rhythm again, Jimmy, □ and the merry-go-round goes round. □ How well you did that together! Sit down for a minute and rest. □ Can you think of some different kinds of booths there might be at a fair? □

Phrase your questions so that the children may explore in detail their ideas of booths.

Today I thought we could make up some of our own booths and have a fair. Would you each take a partner, and then join up with another set of partners, so that there are four children in your group. □ Good. Quiet now, and listen carefully for a minute. First, the children in each group can decide among themselves what kind of booth they would like to have, and they can also choose a place to make it in this room. So start to work and set up your booth with some chairs or other things you can find. When your booth is ready, we can begin our fair. Put your thinking caps on, and get to work quickly.

Give the children ample opportunity to sort out their problems for themselves. If they seem lost, guide them by asking some simple questions related to their problem, so that they may make their own decisions. When you see all the booths are nearly ready, clap your hands.

Hurry and finish up your booths, then sit down quietly with your partners. □ Decide in your group who are to be the first set of partners and who will be the second set of partners. □ This time, let's say that the second set of partners stay at the booth and run it, while the first set of partners visit the other booths. All ready. The people in the booths begin to call out what they have to offer, and the other partners start to wander around the fair and visit the booths. You can try or buy anything you find at a booth. □

Do not interrupt the children at work, but join in this exercise by walking around and talking with the children about their booths; your interest helps them to believe in what they are doing. Ask questions which will encourage the children to use their imagination. Some examples of questions are: "Where have you put the prizes?" "Is your cash register over there?" "Were you able to make the right change?" "How do you know if the player has won a prize?" "What were your customers like?" The same kind of question may be asked in a general discussion with the children after the first part of this exercise is done and before you reverse the groups; a discussion of this sort helps to stimulate the children's awareness of the situation, and thus they can create in greater depth the next time they do the drama. When you sense that the children have exhausted the possibilities of the present situation, clap your hands and say:

Return to your own booth, and everybody rest for a few minutes.

Help the children to analyze how well they felt their idea of the booth had worked out during the fair.

Let's keep all these suggestions in our minds when we do it again. This time the first set of partners will stay at the booth, and the second set of partners will visit the other booths. Quickly take your places. ▫ Everyone ready, let's begin the fair. ▫

As soon as they finish their playing of this situation, clap your hands.

Sit down where you are and relax. Did you enjoy it more this time? ▫ It was a wonderful fair with lots of good ideas, wasn't it? Thank you all for your work today; I did enjoy it.

THREE

Theme:

THE CIRCUS

Emphasis:

Developing control of movement

Materials: Drum.
Records.
   SUGGESTED: *Tiger Rag.*
          Mack the Knife.

Gain the children's attention with a loud beat on the drum.

You are all rubber balls. See how high you can bounce to the drumbeat. Ready.

Begin a series of heavy slow beats on the drum, and finish with a loud beat.

And stop. Good. And now see if you can bounce quickly over here to the drumbeat.

Make faster beats. When all the children arrive near you, end the drumming on a loud beat.

You did! Sit down and relax. How many of you have ever been to a circus? □ This afternoon as a special treat we are all going to the circus.

Start the record. (A lively march. Suggested: *Tiger Rag.*)

There it is, over there. Stand up, and off you go to the circus! See the big tent with all the flags flying. Do you hear the music as you go toward it? Oh, look! There are the clowns. Do you think they look sad or funny? And see the jugglers. How many balls are they keeping in the air at the same time? Look, over there is the big top. Buy a ticket and go in to see the three-ring show. How high do you think the tent roof is? Can you see the tightrope

walkers way up in the air? I wonder how they balance themselves. Isn't that the lion tamer down there? How many lions are there in the cage? Look at all the sawdust on the floor of the ring. I'm hungry; can you see a man selling hot dogs? Good, let's buy one and eat it. □ The horses are coming into the ring with the bareback riders. Aren't the horses beautiful? And what costumes are their riders wearing?

Let's go outside again; maybe there are some elephants. Oh, there are! We can help carry some water for them. □ Look, over there are the wagons that the circus people live in and use for their dressing rooms. There's a painted wagon; it has a Punch and Judy show. Let's watch it. Isn't it funny? □ Oh, the show's over. It's time to come back home, over here.

Indicate the place.

Relax on the floor for a few minutes after our big day.

Fade out the record. There follows a discussion with the children on what they saw at the circus. Talk about the lion tamer, the tightrope walkers, the acrobats, the horses, the elephants, and the ticket taker. End the discussion by asking the children:

Do you think the clowns were funny or sad? □ What costumes were the clowns wearing? □ Did anyone see a clown band? □ Let's think what else we saw. What were the wagons like? □ What do you think

happened at the Punch and Judy Show? □ What are puppets? □ Do you know how they are made? How do they work? □

Allow sufficient time for the children's answers to these questions.

You are all puppets!

Start a steady drumbeat and continue it while you explain the following actions to the children.

The puppeteer pulls the string on your head. Your head moves up and down, up and down; he turns it from side to side, right, left, and up and down. □ Now he pulls the string on your elbows: up, down, up, down. □ Now the hands: up, down, up, down. □ Then he pulls the strings on your ankles, one at a time: up, down, up, down. □ The puppeteer pulls all the strings at once and you stand up. □ Now he lets them go, and on the loud drumbeat you flop down. □ Then he pulls you up again, and you can think he pulls the different strings for your head, arms, and legs as you wish, and you dance around. □ Suddenly, plunk!

Loud beat on the drum.

All the strings break, and you fall down in a heap. □ Remember the tightrope walkers? They had to walk along a very straight line, carefully balancing themselves on the rope. You are all tightrope walkers. Stand up and choose a line anywhere on the floor to walk along. Now to the drumbeat carefully walk along that line toward the other side of the room. Got your balance? Ready, and off you go. □

Use a slow, steady beat. After they have gone some distance make a loud beat on the drum.

Good. Stop and turn around. □ Take an umbrella to help you balance this time, and listen carefully. On the loud drumbeat, jump and change direction and walk along your tightrope facing the new way until the next loud drumbeat; then jump and change direction again.

Use a slow, steady beat, varied with several loud beats for the jumping and turning actions.

Good, you did it and nobody fell off. Jump down off the rope and throw your umbrellas away. □ Now form a circle, and you are all circus ponies. Gallop around in a circle to the drumbeat. □

Make some beats on the drum to simulate a gallop,

as: da,da,dum — da,da,dum. End the drumming with a loud beat.

Whoa! This time listen for the drumbeat to change, and as the beat slows down, the ponies stop and paw the ground and move their heads up and down.

For these actions, use the gallop beat and vary it with slow, steady beats. Do this for some time. Then give one loud beat.

All the ponies are tired, and they lie down on the floor and rest. □ You remember the sawdust on the floor in the big top? Put your hand out and feel it; run it through your fingers. □ See how many hand-prints you can make in the sawdust around you. □ The clowns had big hands and feet, didn't they? Suppose we are all funny clowns. Choose any costume you want and put it on. □ Don't forget the big shoes, □ and — oh, yes — take a handful of red balloons. □ Walk around to the drumbeat, and each time the drum stops give a balloon to a child who is at the circus.

For this action produce a continuous marching beat that you stop several times with a very loud beat. Continue this until you say:

This is your last balloon, the biggest one of all. Give it away, □ and now they are all gone. Oh, look! There's your funny car. Chase after it. □ Hold your hat!

Begin a fast beat; then stop the drumming with a loud bang.

On the loud bang, catch the car and climb in. □ Isn't it a funny car? It has no motor, you have to work it with your hands and feet. See if you can make it work. □ You can? Drive it to the music.

Start a record. (A simple, lively rhythm. Suggested: Mack the Knife.)

Don't bump into anyone as you drive around.

The children sit on the floor and, in the rhythm of the music, they work their hands and feet, as if they were in a toy car. After a short while, stop the music.

Now this time sit quietly and listen to the music carefully.

Start the record again.

What instruments can you hear being played? □ Stand up, you are the clown band. March around and play the big drum, □ the trombone, □ and now any instrument that the music suggests to you. □ You are the band conductor. Put down your instruments, and each of you conduct your own clown band. □

When the children have had time to enjoy this experience, fade out the record.

You did that very well. Come over here and sit down for a few minutes and relax. □

Today I thought we could do a story about a circus. It is called "The Red Umbrellas." One night when the circus was in town, all the people were very excited. They bought their tickets and entered the big top, then took their seats and waited for the show to begin.

The clowns were in their dressing room, over there, (Indicate the place.) putting on their make-up and costumes for the show; the ringmaster was in his wagon, over there, (Indicate the place.) and was pulling on his big black boots so that he would be ready to start the show. The tightrope walkers, in the wagon over there, (Indicate another place.) had just finished tying on their pink ballet shoes when they went to get their red umbrellas. The umbrellas could not be found in the dressing room although they searched everywhere for them. So they went to the clowns to ask them if they had seen the umbrellas—maybe they had taken the umbrellas as a joke. But no, no one had seen them. The poor tightrope walkers went to the ringmaster's wagon to tell him their sad story. He had not seen the umbrellas. What were they to do? It was time for the show to start.

The very unhappy tightrope walkers returned to their dressing room. The ringmaster entered the big top and announced in his biggest voice that the great show was about to begin. The first act of the show was to be the clowns. The clowns came riding into the ring in their funny car, and they all got out of it with their instruments. They began to play a clown band number. Then a funny thing happened. Every time the slide trombones were played they made the most peculiar noise. Finally the clowns looked to see what was the matter, and what do you suppose they found? □ The red umbrellas! The clowns took the umbrellas out of the trombones and put them away safely in their funny

car. Then the clowns did their act. As soon as they had finished their act, the clowns got back in their funny car and drove it straight to the dressing room of the tightrope walkers. Phew! they were just in time. The ringmaster was announcing the next number on the program. It was to be the tightrope walkers.

The tightrope walkers were very happy to have their umbrellas, and they went into the ring and did their act so beautifully that everyone in the audience agreed it was the best circus they had ever seen, and they clapped and clapped and clapped. That would be a fun story for us to do together.

As you continue talking, divide the children into three groups of roughly the same size. Indicate the same working areas for the various groups as you did during the story.

This time we will have this group as the clowns, and they can have their dressing room over there. The next group are tightrope walkers, with their dressing room over there. And let's say the rest of you are the audience and can help make the circus ring with some chairs here. John, we need a ringmaster. Would you like to help us out and make your wagon over there? Everyone quickly make your places, and then we will be ready to begin. □

If the groups have any difficulty constructing their "places," help them out. When you see the children have nearly finished their work, clap your hands.

Everybody nearly finished? Sit down quietly in your place and we'll start our story. Let's begin with the audience entering the big top from here.

Indicate a place for the entrance.

Each person takes a seat in the circle around the ring. □ The clowns are in their dressing room putting on their costumes and make-up. □ The ringmaster is in his wagon getting ready for the show, □ and the tightrope walkers are just finishing tying up their shoes. They begin to look for their red umbrellas.

Allow the children to continue with the action of the story in their own way. But if at any time they seem lost in the sequence of the drama, do help them out by suggesting the next action to them. At the finish of the drama, ask the children if they have any ideas of how the story could be improved, or if there is anything they would like to add to it. When the time permits, the story can be done again with the various groups changed about. For the children's enjoyment, you should also incorporate any suggestions they may have made for additions to the story. But begin the story as you did in the previous presentation of it. At the end, thank the children for their work and their ideas during the class.

FOUR

Theme:

THE CAVES

Emphasis:

Developing imagination through movement and language flow

Materials: Drum.
Record.
 SUGGESTED: *La Mer*, Debussy.

With a loud beat on the drum to gain the children's attention, ask them to come and gather around you.
What do you like to do best on a very hot·day in the summer?

Listen to the children's ideas and accept all their answers. Since the one we want to use for the experience today is "swimming," lead them through your interest and questions to give this answer.
It's so hot this afternoon, how about a picnic on the beach? Each one of you, go to your house and make a lunch. □ Now get your swim suits and anything else you might like to take. □ Don't forget a towel! Pack them all in a bag. □ Ready, off we go.

Start the music. (A flowing rhythm suggesting the sea. Suggested: "Play of the Waves," *La Mer*, Debussy.) Allow the children to march around, then indicate a place for the beach, and say:
There's the sand, over there. And here we are at the beach at last. Quickly change your clothes in the dressing rooms, and come out in your bathing suits. □

The sand is so hot on your bare feet, go down to the water's edge and try the water with your toe. Oh, doesn't it feel cool? Let's run in. Last one in's a monkey's uncle! □ There, now we are all wet, let's

swim. □ Some of you are even diving. □ What a wonderful swim, but it's time to come out now. □ Look at the footprints you make as you walk in the sand with your wet feet! Try putting your feet in as many directions as you can. □ Keep your balance.□ There's a piece of smooth wet sand. With your big toe, see if you can write your name in it. □ You did. Now, run and get your towel and dry yourself off. □ See all those shells over there. Let's go and collect some. □ Bring them back here, (Indicate the place.) and we'll sit down and all look at them.

Fade out the music. During the discussion, have the children describe and show the shells they have found.
Carefully put the shells with your things to take home, and now get out your beach ball. □ Ask a friend to play catch with you. □ Toss it to and fro, to and fro. □ Isn't it fun? Don't let the ball go in the water. Oops, some of you did. Quick, get the ball before the waves carry it out into the deep water. □ Good, you rescued it. Better put it back safely with your things. □ Oh, you must be tired and hungry. Get your lunches out, and sit over here where it is cool.

Indicate the place.
Then we'll eat.

With the children, discuss what they have brought for their lunch. What kind of sandwiches did they make? Did they bring any cookies, cakes, or fruit? Discuss various other kinds of goodies that they brought. What did they bring to drink? During the discussion, ask a few of the children to share some of their lunch with you since you didn't have time to make one yourself.

You've all eaten your lunches. Let's put the waste paper in the rubbish can over there. ▢
Indicate the place.

Did anyone think to bring a sand pail or a shovel? ▢ Oh good, go and get them. Then choose a friend, and ask your friend to help you build a sand castle. ▢
Walk among the children and ask them about their sand castles. Some sample questions are: "Are you going to put a moat around it?" "What will you use for a flag?" "How high have you made yours?" "Are those turrets that are on the corners?" "Did you need stones to build a wall around it?" When their attention begins to waver, clap your hands and suggest to them:

Now we'll take a walk along the beach.
Begin a drumbeat in a rhythm that will suit the varied walking actions in the following section.

Isn't that strange? The sand has vanished, and under our feet now there are little stones. ▢ What's that dark opening in the hill over there? Its a cave! ▢ Let's climb up and go in. ▢ Oh, isn't it wet and dark? Feel the slimy walls. Be careful as you walk on the narrow ledge, there's water running down below! ▢ Did you ever try calling in a cave? Try it. Call "Hello." ▢ Does your voice echo? Say "Hello" again. ▢ Look! What are those big shapes moving ahead? I think they may be monsters! What do you think? Can you see them? ▢ Oh, let's get out of here and go back. Quickly get out into the sunshine. ▢ There we are. Isn't it good to be outside again? Go back to the beach. ▢

It's time to go home now. We had better change back into our clothes. ▢ Pick up your bag, and don't forget your shells. Then start for home. ▢
When the children have arrived "home," end the action with a loud beat on the drum. Ask the children to put down their belongings, and then to come back to you and sit down.

Wasn't that scary in the caves? ▢
Have a discussion with the children on the caves, and stress the monsters. Do monsters really exist? Do they exist now? What shapes do the children

imagine monsters to be? What colors? Are the monsters friendly or unfriendly? Be sure to establish that both kinds of monster are possible.

Up on your feet, and you are all monsters who are going to move around to the drumbeat.
Now with a slow, heavy drumbeat suggest to the children that they are several different kinds of monster. Be sure to use the children's ideas of monsters. If it is necessary to stimulate the children's creative powers, you can suggest: beautiful golden spiders with many emerald green legs, creepy green lizards with short black and silver legs, fat round purple turtles with yellow feet, or others you may wish to create out of your imagination.

Each take a partner, and the two of you make up your own monster together. ▢ Good. Now see if you can make your monster move about the room. ▢ Good. Sit down and relax. ▢ John and Joe, you made a very interesting monster together. Would you like to make it again and share your work with us? ▢
Have several pairs of children share their examples of monsters with the rest of the class. When they have finished, thank them. Then continue:

Quickly, all change partners, and each pair decide between you, which one wants to be "A" and which one wants to be "B". Now listen carefully. "B" is a nice monster and tries to make friends with "A", who is a child. But the monster has to make friends with the child using only monster talk. Monster talk can be made up out of any noises you would like to use; the "meaning" comes from the sound of your voice. Begin working together now and see if the monster can make friends with you. ▢
Give the children two minutes to do this exercise and observe them at their work. When they have nearly finished, clap your hands and say:

A very good try. For this story we'll each change places with our partner. This time "A" is the monster and speaks in monster talk. He aims to make friends with "B", who is the child, by trying to give the child a present. ▢
If there were any good examples of the children making effective use of their imagination to create monster talk, ask the pairs involved to share their work with the class. If they do, thank them for their good work and tell them that theirs was most inter-

esting monster talk. Then continue:

Now everyone come over here, and we'll think up a story about some children and some monsters that they meet. Shall we begin with a group of children who are playing on the beach? □ And then let's say that they see a cave and decide to explore it. When they finally reach the darkest part of the cave, they find some jewels. But they don't know that these jewels are guarded by monsters, who at this time have fortunately fallen asleep. The children take the jewels and run out of the cave to look at them in the sunlight. They try to decide on a place to hide the jewels. Some of the children begin to think that it wasn't very honest to steal the jewels, and that they should take them all back again into the cave. While the children are crawling back into the cave, the monsters wake up. They find their jewels are missing, and they all become sulky and cross. When the monsters see the children coming back with the jewels, at first they are unfriendly. But when the children show them that they want to return the jewels, the monsters make friends with them. The monsters give each child a special present to take home.

Now, for our story, we'll need some children and some monsters. Let's see who we have for our monsters.

Place any children who volunteer in the specific group of their choice, and then divide up the rest of the children so that there are two groups of equal size.

Each of you in the monster group can decide what kind of monster you are and what you look like, and we'll have all the monsters build their cave over

here.

Indicate the place.

All the children will have this place for the beach on which they are playing when the story starts.

Indicate the place.

The children have to think about what games they are playing on the beach and what kinds of jewels they are going to find.

If necessary, assist the children in the creation of their cave; but help them build it from their ideas. When all the children are ready, begin the drama. The monsters are asleep in the cave. The children begin to play on the beach.

Help the children with additional narration only if the action seems to be faltering. Give any such help in the form of a suggestion that will stimulate the children to remember the next happening in the story. When the children have finished playing out the drama, ask all of them, wherever they are, to sit down on the floor.

How well you did that story! Can you think of anything we can add to it that will help make it an even better story when we do it again? □

Listen to the children's suggestions and incorporate as many ideas as you can into the basic outline for the story. Ask the class if they would like to change their roles; if they would, have the children become the monsters and the monsters become the children. Begin the story again with the monsters being asleep and the children playing on the beach. Then let them play out their version of the drama. At the end of the lesson thank all the class for so much good work together, and thank them for all the interesting ideas they added to the story.

Theme:

THE FIRE

Emphasis:

Awareness of climax and de-climax

Materials: Drum, cymbal.
Record.
SUGGESTED: *Firebird Suite*, Stravinsky.

With a loud beat on the drum, ask the children to come and sit near you on the floor. Then use a cymbal and strike it several times to produce a clanging sound.

What does that sound remind you of?

You may get suggestions such as a school bell or a clock; if so, ask:

In the street, what would make a noise like that? □ Yes, a fire engine. Do you hear it?

Produce the clanging sound again.

There goes a fire engine now. Let's follow it to the fire.

Start the record. (A fast, exciting rhythm building to a climax. Suggested: *Firebird Suite*, Stravinsky.)

Away you go. See where all the traffic is stopped. There it is. Is there a big crowd around? How many fire engines have come? Do they have extension ladders? How do the firemen unreel their hoses? How do they attach them to the hydrants? □ What are the firemen wearing? □ Is the fire in a house? An apartment? A garage? Where is it? □ How high are the flames? □ Can you smell the smoke? □ Can you see the smoke? Look and see if there are any people inside. How are they saved? □

The fire is finally put out. Was the building badly burned? □ The fire engines leave the scene. Look around; everyone has left now. The fire is all over. Leave and come back here.

Indicate the place, and end the music.

Sit on the floor and relax.

Discuss with the children the experiences they have imagined at the fire, using questions such as those from the narrative to stimulate their thinking. When the discussion nears its end, proceed:

Each of you lie down straight on the floor with lots of room around you. □ You are a wooden match. On the loud crashing sound, your head will be struck

Loud crash on the cymbal.

and you burst into flame.

With a steady drumbeat, which becomes slower and slower, suggest:

Listen to the drumbeat, as the flames move around your shoulders, your arms, your body, your knees, and right down to your toes, and the f-l-a-m-e d-i-e-s o-u-t.

End the drumbeat.

Good. Now let's try it again.

Repeat the match exercise to the same drumbeat as before.

Much better. This time curl up in a small ball lying on the floor. □ You are a spark of fire, carelessly tossed on the ground. When the drumbeat starts, the wind fans you into flame.

Continue talking and with a rhythm appropriate to

the action, start the drumbeat. This exercise is done to a steady beat that becomes louder and louder as it builds up to the climax; and then the sound gradually diminishes to become silent, the de-climax.

Then, while you are still lying on the ground, you grow, and grow, and grow into a big flame. □ Some one sees the flame and pours water on you, and you gradually become smaller and smaller and smaller again, □ and t-h-e f-l-a-m-e d-i-e-s o-u-t.

End the drum beats.

We'll do it again.

Start the steady drumbeats again. Continue talking while you build the drumbeats up to the climax, followed by the de-climax, in the same way as in the previous exercise.

This time, as you grow bigger and bigger, you stand up. □ The wind tosses you about, and you become a bigger and wider flame, and you spread all around the room. □ Then the wind dies down, and you are dropped onto the ground. □ And you get smaller and smaller until all your f-l-a-m-e i-s o-u-t.

End the drum beats.

And you are just a tiny cinder.

Now everyone crouch down on your hands and knees. □ You are each a little flame that has started from an electric outlet.

Suggest what the children are to do at the same time as you beat the rhythm. The rhythm used is a steady, slow beat. The sound gradually builds in volume to the climax, which is followed with a crash on the cymbal.

You creep slowly and slowly along the floor; □ then you come to a wall, and you grow bigger and bigger and bigger □ until the fireman's hose drenches you with water and you fall all at once to the floor—and you are out!

Crash on the cymbal.

How quickly the firemen put you all out.

Divide the children into two groups and give each group a space in which to work.

Now you are the firemen at a fire station. The alarm sounds.

Strike the cymbal several times.

Quickly put on your uniforms, your boots, your hats and rubber coats. □ All stand close together near your fire engine. □ As soon as you can, jump onto it. Now that you are on the engine, be careful that you don't fall off as the engine speeds out of the fire station and down the street to the fire.

Repeatedly strike the cymbal for the bell on the fire engine, and allow enough time for the children to have a good ride before you continue the story.

You've arrived at your fire. Quickly get off the engine, and unwind and attach the hoses to the hydrants. □ Put up the ladders, and climb them with the hoses. □ Aim the hoses at the fire, and pour the water on the burning building. □ I think the flames are out now. Roll up the hoses, and put them back on the fire engine. □ Look, there is someone at the top window. Get out the big safety net.

Everybody stand in a circle; each fireman must hold on to the edge of the net. □ Hold it tight. You shout to the person to jump. □

For the following action, use a steady drumbeat, and build up the volume to a very loud beat.

You wait, and you wait, and finally with a crash the person jumps.

Good, he isn't hurt. You have saved him. Put the net back on the truck, and now go into the house and explore it to see what damage has been done. □ Walk carefully over the fallen wood and through the water. □ It is hard to see with all the smoke still inside. You hear a noise. □ See if you can find out what made it. There it is. Do something to help. □ And now come out of the house again. □ The fire is over now. Get on your fire engines, and drive slower this time back through the streets to the station. □ At the station, park the truck and take off your uniforms. □ Sit down and relax.

Begin a discussion on the children's experiences as firemen. Especially, ask several of the children to say what made the noise they heard in the house, and what they did to help. When they went into the house, was there much damage from the fire? As their interest wanes, produce a loud beat on the drum and say:

Stand up and find a place in the centre of the floor. □ You are a person who is in a burning house. To the drumbeat, begin walking to try to get out of it. □

Start a steady drumbeat.

Listen, and on the loud drumbeat, stop walking. □

Make a loud beat.

There is a door in front of you. Open the door. □
The room beyond it is filled with smoke. Close the
door again. □

Turn and

*Begin to make the steady beats slightly louder and
faster.*

start walking again another way. □ Stop on the loud
beat.

Loud beat.

Open that door. □ No, that room is all smoke too.
Close the door. □ Turn and

Begin to make the steady beats still louder and faster.

start walking straight ahead. Don't be frightened. □
On the crash of the cymbal you will find the front
door. □

*Strike the cymbal for the climax. Then continue the
drumbeats for the following.*

There it is, open the door. □ It is the outside. Run
out of the house; □ then stand and take in big
breaths of fresh air. In-out, in-out, in-out. □

Fade the drumbeat out.

You did that very well. Nobody panicked, and you
reached the outside safely.

*Use the same rhythm as in the above exercise,
building the drumbeats in intensity to the final
crash on the cymbal. Begin a steady beat on the
drum and say:*

Now this time you are in the burning house again,
and you walk and walk, □ then —

Loud beat on the drum.

Good, you remembered to stop. Now open the
door. □ Close it again; you can't get out that way. □
Turn and start walking in another direction. □

*On the drum make a series of faster beats and follow
them with one loud beat for the children to stop.*

There is a door in front of you. You try hard to open
it, but it is stuck. □ Turn and start walking upstairs. □
Go to the window.

Make some fast beats on the drum.

Open the window, and call for help. □ The firemen
have a net below. On the loud cymbal crash, JUMP
to safety.

Loud crash of the cymbal.

Crawl out of the net. □ Move your wrists to see if

they are broken; □ try your arms; □ move your
head, □ your waist. □ Keep them all moving as you
try one leg and then the other leg. □ You are all O.K.
Good. Collapse on the ground.

Discuss with the children how fires could start.
From this discussion have the children choose one
idea, and from this idea help them to make up a
story about a fire. As an example, you might suggest
that they begin their story with some people in a
house; then allow the children to decide who the
people in the house are. Then let the story develop
until the start of a fire. Then you might say, "Now
someone will have to call the fire department. Who
will it be?"

Accept for the outline one of the children's suggestions. Continue the story by suggesting that the
flames begin to grow bigger and the fire spreads
around the house. The fire department arrives. How
do you think we should have the firemen put out
the flames and rescue the people?

For these actions in the story, choose some good
ideas suggested by the children. How do we end
the story?

For the end of the story, decide on the most popular
idea offered by the children. Divide the children
into three groups: "A" group are the people in the
house, "B" group are the flames, and "C" group are
the firemen. Decide with the children's help where
the house and the fire station are located. Designate
an area for each group to work in. Ask the children
to start making their "buildings." When these are
ready, allow the children to play out their own story.
A music background helps to control the action, but
you must be sensitive to the volume required in
relation to the dialogue and the action of the
children.

Have a discussion after they have finished playing
out the story. Ask the children for any ideas they
might like to add. If time permits, select some of
these suggestions to use when the story is repeated.
For the playing of the new version of the story, if
it is desirable, change around the roles of the three
groups. At the end of the lesson thank the class for
their good work.

SIX

Theme:

A TIGER HUNT

Emphasis:

Improving listening ability

Materials: Drum.
Record.
  SUGGESTED: *Carnival of the Animals*, Saint-Saëns.

Come and form a big circle. Now, standing in
your place, make any movements you want to the
drumbeat until I make a very loud beat, and then
see if you can hold the position you are in and
all become ice statues.
Beat any fast rhythm, ending with one loud beat.
What good statues you made! Let's do it again and
on the loud beat I will say, "Freeze!"
Beat another rhythm, then give a loud beat and say:
Freeze! □ Good. Again, move around to the
drumbeat until you hear the loud beat and "Freeze."
Make a slower beat, then give a loud beat and
say:
Freeze! □ Oh, you are listening well! Sit down and
relax. □ If you heard a loud drum beat and I said
"Freeze," no matter what work you were doing,
what do you think you should do?
After a few of their answers:
That's right; stop whatever you are doing, stand
still, and listen. Let's see how well it works.
Take a partner, and all walk in a big circle to the
drumbeat and talk to each other.
Beat a marching rhythm; end it with a loud beat
and say:
Freeze! □ That was quite good, but maybe one or

two weren't listening quite hard enough when I
said "Freeze." Turn around and go the other way,
and let's all try to stop together this time.
Beat a march on the drum, then end with a loud
beat and say:
Freeze! □ Good work. During any of the lessons,
if you hear me say "Freeze," remember to stop
just like that.
Now all face into the centre, sit down, and think
of a nursery rhyme. When I clap my hands, begin
to say out loud the rhyme you have thought of, all
speaking at the same time.
Clap your hands, then after a short time, strike a
loud beat on the drum and say:
Freeze! □ Was anyone able to hear what rhyme
anybody else was saying?
One or two of the children may say "yes" but most,
or all, of the class will answer "no."
It is hard to hear what other people are saying when
you are talking yourself.
Select three children.
Now let's have a game. We'll ask only these three
children to tell us their names and where they live,
and they must all say it at the same time, when I
clap my hands. The rest of us will listen. Begin,
my name is . . . .
Clap your hands for the children to begin.
Thank you. Although we listened hard, were we
able to hear what each one was telling us? Think;

did you really hear what street Mary lived on? Could you tell us her address? □

Again the general answer should be "no."

Now everybody listen, and I will tell you where I live. I live at 128 Yonge Street. Can each of you tell me where I live? Say it together. □ That shows that you all listened very carefully. Now, in a group, if we really want to hear what other people are saying, or telling us, how many people should speak at once? □

The answer should be a chorus of "one."

That's right. Only one. And what do the other people who are with them do? □ They listen. Let's try, as we are sitting here, for each one, in turn around the circle, to say the name of his favorite fruit. I'll start: "pineapple." □ What a lot of different names of fruits we heard! That was because we listened.

Now, everyone stand up. □ You are going to walk anywhere around the room to the drumbeat. When you begin to walk, make as much noise with your feet as you can; and when the drumbeat gets softer, gradually walk more quietly with each step until I can't hear one footstep. Let's try it.

Begin a marching beat on the drum.

Don't forget to listen for the drumbeats!

If the children are too boisterous, make a loud bang on the drum and say "Freeze!" Wait for them to stop.

Let's try again; not too many of you were listening.

Do the exercise again, and gradually fade the drumbeats. Then make a loud beat for them to stop.

That was quite well done. Now let's do it the other way around. Begin to walk very softly, then walk making louder footsteps. Listen for the drumbeats to get gradually louder, and I will say "Freeze" on the last loud beat.

Begin to beat the drum softly, then increase the volume. Build it up to a very loud beat and say:

Freeze! You did it much better that way. Now see if we can all do as well if we go from walking loudly to walking softly. Listen to the drum to help you.

Beat the drum to a walking rhythm, gradually decreasing the volume. Add one beat more for "stop."

Yes, that was much better this time. Lie down on the floor where you are. □ Everybody be as still as you can, and see if you can hear your own heartbeat. Quiet, and listen very carefully. □ How many did hear their heartbeat? □ Now all be very quiet and listen to the sounds that you can hear outside this room. Don't say anything yet, but see if you can think what is making the sounds you hear. □ Everyone keep as quiet as possible, and I will walk around and touch you when it is your turn to answer. Then I'll ask you a question about the sounds you can hear outside the room.

Walk among the children, lightly touching various ones with the drumstick. Ask such questions as:

What kind of sound did you hear? Did you know what made it? Did you hear a different sound? What do you think it was? Was there a sharp noise? What was that made by? Was there a continual noise? How do you think it was made? Did you hear any traffic sounds? Could you tell what kind of vehicle on the road would make a sound like that? Did you hear any airplane sounds? Can you tell me another sound you heard? What kind of sound was it? What would have made it? Any other sounds that we haven't mentioned? Raise your hand quietly. What is the noise? Is it still going on? Everyone listen and see if you can hear it too. □ Good. Any other sounds? Where do you think the sound came from?

Return to the drum and give a loud beat to gain their attention.

Sit up where you are. □ We have been listening to the sounds of a big city. Have any of you seen any movies or television programs about a jungle? □ A lot of you have. Does a jungle have the same sounds as a city? □ Does a jungle have any traffic noises? □ How do people mostly get around in the jungle? □ That's right, they walk; and usually they walk in a line one behind the other because the paths are very narrow and overgrown with the thick trees and plants. How do you suppose people carry their food and camping supplies into the jungle?

Accept the children's answers, and then suggest to them:

Do you think it might be a good idea to carry supplies on your head while you walk, in the same way as the people do who live in the jungle? □ Today, let's all go for a walk into the jungle and carry our supplies to a camp. As we go along, listen for all the different sounds you can hear in the jungle, and try to think what would be making these sounds. Remember, it is very hot and there are a great many wild animals who live in the jungle. Be very quiet when you walk, or they will hear you coming. Quickly get into groups of eight. □ Line up ready for the journey and lift your share of the supplies up on your head to carry them. □ All ready, start off.

Begin the record. (A rhythmic march, suggesting jungle atmosphere. Suggested: Parts 1-4, *Carnival of the Animals,* Saint-Saëns.)

All stay close together in your group: you may need to help each other. □ Don't get your feet tangled in the long vines on the path. Did you hear that bird screech? Can you see him? What size and color is he? □ Can you see that big green branch of the tree moving? Do you think there is an animal swinging in the tree? □ You can talk to the other people in your line, but always remember to keep your voices very low. □

What was that rustling noise ahead? Quiet! Don't make a sound. □ Your leader signals you to stop walking. □ Carefully, put your bundles on the ground. □ Sh, sh. Some of your group should go and find out what it is you heard. □ You may be in great danger from one of the wild animals. Everyone be very quiet. □ Now your friends come back and tell you what they have found. □ What is the danger? Quick! Make a decision and do something about it. □

Phew! The danger is over. Lift up your bundles again and continue on your way to the camp. □ It gets hotter as you go along; and there seem to be so many different sounds you can hear all the time. How happy you are when your leader finally signals that the camp is just ahead! □ Take the last few steps, and collapse on the floor when you reach camp.

Fade out the music.

What a wonderful adventure!

Discuss with the children the happenings on their trip. Some questions you might ask are:

What was the rustling sound your group heard? What was the monkey (or other animal) doing? What did you do about the noise you heard? What other animal did you hear on your trip? Where was he? Was it a bird that made the screeching sound? What color was he? Was it a big bird making all that noise? What did the trees sound like when you brushed them aside as you walked along? Did you hear any other strange noises? What did you think made them? Were you frightened? What did you do when you thought you were in danger?

Continue to encourage the children to talk about the jungle and its sounds until they begin to lose interest. End the discussion by saying:

What sounds would lions and tigers make when they walk through the jungle? □ To the drumbeat, you are all tigers moving through the jungle.

Begin a light, rather slow beat.

Look around and see if there are any people on the path as you go. □ Better keep out of their way, or they might shoot you. □

You are all lions now, going down to the river to get a drink. Move very stealthily. □ Listen to hear if anyone is coming. □ No. Have a drink, and then go back carefully to your lion's den. □ Curl up and have a nice sleep. □

Make a loud beat on the drum.

Everyone wake up! You are children again! Come over here and sit down. □

Today we are going to do a story about a tiger hunt. Because tigers are very clever, dangerous animals, the only way people can hope to hunt them is to try and be smarter than a tiger.

First, they look for a place near some water where they think a tiger may be living. Then the hunters put some raw meat on the ground for the tiger to find, and they hide themselves nearby to watch what happens. They keep very quiet. When a tiger comes to the meat, the hunters don't try to shoot it then because the tiger might attack them. Instead, they wait quietly until the tiger has had his dinner, and they watch as he goes off to his home for a long sleep.

While he is asleep, the hunters build a tree house above the place where he had his dinner, high up in the trees. They make it higher than a tiger can jump; and when the tree house is ready, the hunters climb up into it, sit very quietly and wait. They know that, when the tiger wakes up, he will go to the water for something to drink. And then he will go in search of more food, and he will always look in the place where he had his last meal for any scraps that he might have left. It is then the hunters are able to shoot the tiger.

But they have to aim very well the first time, or the tiger may start to attack their tree house. Sometimes more tigers come to join in the attack, and the hunters are in great danger. If the people are lucky, the tigers go away and they can escape; or if there are other hunters in a camp close by, they will come when they hear a call for help and save their friends. People who want tigers for zoos also use tree houses to wait in until they can trap the animals in big nets. Then these people take the tigers back to their camp and keep them there until they can be taken out of the jungle.

How would you like to make up your own tiger hunt? □ If there are four tigers in each group and four hunters, I think that would be a good team for your work together. Divide up into groups of eight. □ In your groups decide who each person is in the story, and think how you are going to work out your ideas for a tiger hunt. You will have ten minutes to do your own story. This group can work over there.

Indicate the place.

The other group will work here.

Indicate the place. If you have more than two groups, give the remainder their working areas also. Divide equally among the groups the chairs, desks, or other equipment so that the children in each

group are able to build a tree house. Help them get to work. Ask questions that will lead them to explore their own ideas for the hunt. Walk among the children to observe their work in action, but don't interrupt them. Let them try to solve most of their own problems. The ten minutes is an arbitrary measure of time; when you feel their concentration is good, extend it. When their interest in the drama seems to have run its course, clap your hands twice, and give them a minute to finish their story. At the end of a minute, make a loud drumbeat.

Freeze! Sit down where you are.

If there has been a good example of a group working out their story together, ask that group to share their work with the rest of the class. You might say to that group:

You were doing some very interesting work, would you like to share it with us? We will all listen quietly.

At the end of the happening, say:

Thank you. See how each one in the group helped to make a good story by listening and then doing his part.

If time permits, continue with:

Would the groups like to do it again? This time switch around the roles of tigers and hunters in your groups, and try to think of another idea you can work out together. Get to work quickly; there is only five minutes left of our time.

Observe them at work. Clap your hands and say:

One minute to finish! □

Make a loud drumbeat and say:

Freeze!

What a lot of good work you have done today. Thank you.

SEVEN

Theme:

THE PRINCESSES' PEARLS

Emphasis:

Developing group sensitivity

Materials: Drum.
Record.
SUGGESTED: *Carnival of the Animals*, Saint-Saëns.

Each child find a place on the floor and lie down. □
Have lots of space around you so that you will be
able to move about easily without touching each
other. Close your eyes and think of a bird's nest. □
Now look into the nest and see some bird's eggs in
it. What color and shape are they? □ See if you can
curl your body up very small. □ Good. Now think
you are a little bird all curled up inside an egg. On
the drumbeats you are going to begin to crack the
shell.
Start a slow beat on the drum.
Crack it open little by little, □ until you come right
out of the shell.
Make a loud beat.
Open your eyes and look at the color of your
feathers; see what a beautiful bird you are! □ Now
test your wings to see if they will flap up and
down. □ Try them again. □ Good, they work very
well. To the music, start to fly around the countryside.
Start the record. (Light and rhythmic, with bird
sounds. Suggested: ''The Cuckoo'' and ''The Aviary,''
from *Carnival of the Animals*, Saint-Saëns.)
Isn't it wonderful how light you feel? Look at your
wings moving up and down so smoothly and easily.
It hardly takes any effort to fly. □

You begin to feel a little hungry; I wonder what
birds eat. □ Worms, that's it. Land on the ground
and look around for some food. □There you see a
lovely white crust. Start to peck at it and eat it. □
As you are eating, you notice a mound of earth
close by, almost like a small hill. It is all full of little
holes, and there are a lot of tiny black creatures
running in and out. What do you suppose they are,
and what are they doing? □
Now you have finished your bread, start to fly
again. □ You begin to look around for somewhere
you can get a drink. There is a big blue surface
ahead on the ground. Land near it and find out
what it is. □ It's water! Have a nice drink. □ I wonder
what those birds are that have white feathers and
can float on the water. □ See how they move around?
Sometimes they dive under the water. It might be
fun to do that, but it's wonderful to be able to fly
around and see so many different sights. Fly way
up high in the blue sky. □ Fly around all the tree
tops and find a nice branch to settle on for a rest. □
You hear a buzzing sound: z-z-z-z. What's that
yellow-and-black-striped little ball with wings?
What is it? □ It is taking something out of the flowers
and going back to a cone-shaped house where
there are a lot of its friends working too, buzzing
in and out of the house. It is nice to be a bird and
not to have to work so hard.
Fly around the country past the farms. □ Zoom low

26

over the fences. □ Isn't it fun? Let's do it again. Zoom low, and then fly way up high again. □ Look at all the other different kinds of birds flying around you. □ Maybe all the birds should fly over the wall into this beautiful garden here and take a rest. □

Indicate the place.

You are so tired from all your flying that you shut your eyes. □ Then the sound of the drum wakes you, and you are all boys and girls again.

Give a loud drumbeat. Then discuss with the children their experiences as birds, the colors of their feathers, and the various kinds of birds they were. Ask them what they felt like when they were flying, and what they saw. Compare birds flying to the ducks swimming on the pond. Ask the children about the little black creatures—what they were and what they were doing. Ask about the fuzzy black-and-yellow-striped insects—what they were and what they were doing. When the children were birds, did they see any other interesting sights during their travels? End the discussion by asking the children if they saw any farm animals and, if so, what the animals were doing.

To a drumbeat, suggest that the children are various farm animals.

You are work horses pulling a wagon loaded with hay. □ You are all pigs rooting around in the barnyard. □ What else?

Using the children's ideas, suggest to them that they are one or two other animals. You might use:

Cows? Yes, big brown and white cows munching lots of green grass. □

End this exercise by saying:

Now, you are all ducks waddling down to the pond for a swim. □ Yes, you can quack if you want to. □ Now you are at the water's edge, go in for a little swim on the pond. □ Good. Quickly get into groups of four. □

Join pairs of groups together, to make sets of eight. Place each set so that it has enough space to work freely.

You are all ants. Get down on the floor and huddle together to make an ant hill. □ Good. Now, to the drumbeat, scurry out to get food. □

Use a fast drumbeat.

Just one tiny piece at a time and hurry back to your home. □ Try not to bump into each other. Work well together. Each one is busy gathering as much food as he can for the family. □

Give sufficient time for the children to become involved with the project. Then:

There, this is the last trip home, and you all huddle back in the ant hill again. □

End the drum.

Good, you were working very well together.

Now choose a leader for each set of eight.

All the leaders are the queen bees in the hive, and all the rest of the group are the worker bees. Each group form together a nice rounded hive around the queen bee. □ There are some very well made hives. Notice how you helped make the hive and where your place is in it. In a moment, all you worker bees are going to gather nectar from some flowers around the room; when you come back, try to take that exact place again. Off you go!

Start a quick drumbeat.

Fly around to all the blossoms and flowers. □

Give the children a few minutes for this work.

Now all fly back to your hive and take up your position.

When all the children are back in position, stop the drumbeats.

A few out of place! Try to think very hard where you are standing, and in what position you have your hands and feet, and this time see if we can work together in the group to help each other do it well. Buzz anywhere around the room and get your nectar from lots of flowers.

Start some quick drumbeats.

Fly up and see if the blossoms on the trees have any nectar in them. □ You have gathered a great deal of nectar this time; now fly back into your beehive. □

End the drum.

How well you worked together to make the beehive again!

With sharp rap on drum, say:

Now all come over here and sit down. I know a good story that we can do about a hive of bees and some princesses.

In a country far away, there was a family that had a house near a beautiful castle. There were three children in the family, two younger sisters, who were really quite mean girls, and an older brother, who was a kind boy. He loved his sisters and often used to play with them. One day the brother offered to take his sisters for a long walk in the country. The girls wanted to go with him and promised to be good children, so off they started. First of all they came to an ant hill, with ants scurrying all over the place gathering food. They stopped to look at them. After a while both the sisters said almost at once, "Let's step all over the ant hill and break it down." The brother stopped them from doing that and said to his sisters, "I will not let you harm the ants." The girls remembered their promise to be good, so they left the ants alone and continued their walk.

Soon they came to a lovely pond with some ducks swimming and diving in it. The children sat down and watched them. It was fun for a short time but the girls had another idea. They jumped up and said, "Let's gather some stones and throw them at the ducks." The brother jumped up quickly, and what do you think he said? ◻ That's right. He said, "No. I will not let you harm the ducks." The girls put down the stones and left the ducks swimming peacefully on the pond. Then the three children went on with their walk.

Suddenly they heard a loud buzzing: z-z-z-z-z. What do you suppose it was? ◻ Not just one bee, but a whole hive of bees on the low fence ahead of them. They ran over to look at the bees. What a lot of honey the bees have made! The girls cried, "Let's build a fire; then we can smoke the bees out and take the honey." The brother was shocked at his sisters, and what did he say to them? ◻ That's what he said: "I will not let you harm the bees." He was angry with his sisters and said that they must return home with him.

He decided to take them back the short way past the castle. When they came near it, they saw a peculiar sight. All the horses in the yard were neighing and pawing the ground and nodding their heads toward the castle door. The brother saw that something was wrong, and he and his sisters quickly went inside the castle. What a strange sight they saw there! All the servants were asleep on the floor; the king and queen were asleep at the table; and no amount of gentle shaking would wake up any of them.

What could the children do to help? Do you suppose they could look around the room for a clue? ◻ Yes, that is just what they did, and they found a clue. In the king's hand they found a note he had been writing. It read, "Find in the garden the hundred pearls belonging to the princesses." The sisters offered to go and find them while the brother stayed to guard the castle.

He waited and waited until it was almost dark. At last the sisters returned. They had looked and looked everywhere in the garden, but when they counted the pearls they had found, they had ten between them. The girls gave them to their brother, who put them in his pocket. Then the sisters were so very tired, that they lay down on the floor and soon were in a deep sleep.

The brother walked around and around trying to think what he should do. Then he saw another note on a desk. It read, "The key to the princesses' room is at the bottom of the pond nearby." What do you think he should do? ◻ That was just what he did. He went to the pond and there he saw the ducks, whom he had saved from harm, swim around and then dive down into the water. When they came up again, what do you think one of the ducks had in his bill? ◻ The golden key! The ducks swam over to the edge of the pond and dropped it at the brother's feet. Quickly he picked it up and thanked the ducks. Then he ran the fastest way back to the castle through the garden.

As he ran, he thought he saw something white on the ground, and he stopped to pick it up. It was a pearl! There was another one over there! Then the brother saw what was happening. All the ants whom he had saved were scurrying back and forth bringing him pearls. He picked them up, counting them as he put them in his pocket, and before long he had counted to a hundred pearls. How grateful he was to the ants for helping him!

He thanked the ants, dashed back to the castle, and unlocked the princesses' door with the golden key. There he found all the princesses in a deep sleep. It was puzzling. He had found all the pearls and still nobody woke up.

Suddenly he heard a buzzing sound. He looked up at the window, and what do you think he saw? □ The queen bee and all the worker bees were flying into the room and each of the workers was bringing some honey. They put it in a large bowl nearby and then they did a very funny thing. The bees buzzed around the sleeping princesses. The brother had an idea. He took some honey with a spoon and put it on the lips of one of the princesses. She started to wake up; she ate up the whole teaspoonful of honey, and after that she woke right up. This then was the way to wake up all the people in the castle. The brother asked the first princess to help. They went to each of the other princesses in the room and woke her up. Then they all went to the throne room and gave a teaspoonful of honey to each of the sleeping people there. Soon everyone was awake again. The king was so grateful to the brother, he shook his hand and thanked him.

It was then that something jingled in the boy's pocket. What do you suppose he had forgotten all about? □ The pearls. He put them on the table, exactly one hundred. The king was overjoyed because the pearls had been a present from the princesses' fairy godmother. The king announced a feast in honor of the good brother who had saved them all, and everyone joined in the party.

Isn't that a long story we are going to do today? Quickly get into groups of four, and then we can begin.

Choose three children from one group for the roles of the brother and the two sisters, and designate a place for the family to build their house. Then ask the extra child from that group to join the next group, which will consist of the king, the queen, and three servants. Give this group a place in which to build the throne room of the castle. Assign the next group of four to be the princesses. If there are any boys among these children, exchange them for girls from the remaining group. Ask the princesses to make their room in the castle next to the throne room. The last group is the bees, and ask them to choose a place to make their beehive. These children can also be the horses for one part of the story, and so suggest to them that they make the courtyard and the castle door in front of the throne room. Give the groups about five minutes to complete their preparations; help them only when necessary.

Now, the princesses, the king and queen and their servants, the three children, and the bees — all take your places for the start of our story. □

Clap your hands and wait for silence.

Good, but what other creatures in the story have we forgotten all about? □ Of course, the ants and the ducks! Would the princesses help us out for that part of the story and be the ducks in a pond over there? □

Indicate a place.

Thank you. Maybe the group in the castle who are the king, queen, and servants could help us and be the ants as well; and they can have their ant hill over there. □

Indicate another place.

Thank you. Everybody be very quiet, and we will start our story with the children in the house waking up in the morning. □

Proceed with the drama, allowing the children to use their own dialogue. If they seem lost at any time, try to interject a question, relating to the narrative, which will lead them to the next happening.

Note: If you have a larger class than 16 there is no need to have any of the children do two parts, and various groups in this story could be made larger to enable all your children to be working at the same time. If time permits, or if you wish to extend this unit for another session, the children will enjoy changing groups and doing it over again. It has a great deal of material for them to remember and is quite a challenge for their minds.

EIGHT

Theme:

LANDING ON THE MOON

Emphasis:

Awareness of space relationships

Materials: Drum.
Records.
    SUGGESTED: *I'm Forever Blowing Bubbles*
                2001: A Space Odyssey
                (theme from soundtrack).

Begin with a loud beat on the drum. Appoint four children to be leaders by saying:

Mary, John, Peter, and Susan, come and stand over here at this end of the room.

Place these children equidistant from each other across the end of the room.

And the rest of you, quickly line up behind these children in even lines. □ Good. Now quiet.

Clap your hands and continue:

You are all airplanes standing on the runway waiting to take off. What happens when airplanes are flying and they crash into each other? □ Yes all those things might happen, they might . . . .

Repeat one or two ideas given by the children, and add:

And then, they fall to the ground. We are going to see what clever airplanes you can be, and try not to crash into each other as you zoom through the air around the room. A loud drumbeat will be a signal for the plane at the front of each line on the runway to take off. Listen. All ready.

After four rather rapid light beats, make the fifth one loud and sustained. Continue this rhythm until

all the children have ''taken off,'' and then continue beating a rapid rhythm as they zoom around.

That's right. Always look where you are going, and make sure that you keep enough space around you.

If there are a few crashes, suggest that: ''Maybe you aren't damaged too badly, see if you can fly safely back to the airport and land on your runway.''

Now all the planes have to prepare for landing. On the loud beat, try to land on your runway one after the other, in whatever order you wish.

When they have all landed, stop the drumbeat.

You did that quite well; let's do it again. This time see if we can keep *all* the planes zooming safely through the air. Prepare for take-off, and listen for your signal.

Repeat the exercise, using the same rhythm on the drum as before.

Always look for a clear space to fly in. Zoom up . . . and down, and tilt from side . . . to side. □ Now begin to look for an airport, anywhere in the room that you want to land. □ There is the runway ahead; prepare for landing. Zoom on to it; put on the brakes; and come to a stop. □ Now that you are safely on the ground, lie there and rest. You are all boys and girls again. Listen to this music.

Start the record. (A light, floating rhythm. Suggested: *I'm Forever Blowing Bubbles*.) And say:

You are lying on the grass; it is a lovely summer day; the sun is warm, and there is a soft breeze blowing. Lie there, and look up at the clouds. They are all white and fluffy. See how they float so easily and smoothly through the sky. □ Even the jetplane looks very small way up in the sky, and it hardly seems to be moving at all. □

Watch that butterfly; he looks such a tiny speck up there. □ He begins to fly in circles down toward the earth and lands very gently on the back of your hand. □ Being careful not to disturb the butterfly from its place on your hand, slowly sit up and look at it. □ What color is it? Does it have any circles or lines on its wings? Are they different colors? How big are the wings? Do they look soft? □

Gently get up and walk around the room with the butterfly still on the back of your hand. □ He likes resting on your hand. Keep your hand nice and steady, and don't let anyone else bump into it. □ Now the butterfly begins to flap his wings up and down; I think he wants to fly away again. Slowly lift up your hand and help him on his journey. □ There he goes! Doesn't he look pretty floating through space? □

Fade out the record. Clap your hands.

Everyone stand still just where he is. Tell me; how many of you have ever blown soap bubbles? □ A lot of you. Have you ever blown them with a pipe? Through a ring? □ You have. Isn't it fun to blow and blow until the bubbles get bigger and bigger? Well, each of you take your pipe or ring, and dip it in the soapy water, and blow the biggest bubble you can. □ What big bubbles! They are as big as you are! Put down your pipe. Open the bubble gently with both hands and step inside it. □

Fade in the record softly again.

Feel all around the inside of it. □ The sun comes out and shines on your bubble, which makes many varied colors and different shapes for you to see. Trace gently with your fingertips some of the shapes on the inside of your bubble. □ Some of the lines go right down to the ground. Some of them curve all the way up over your head and around as far as you can reach. □

Now a breeze comes along and lifts you and your bubble up into space. □ You drift up and down. The breeze twirls you lightly around. □ You float and turn, and float and turn; then your bubble comes gently to rest on the ground. □ Part your bubble again, and come out of it. □ Walk around it, for one last look. □ Then take a pin and prick it. Bang. All that is left of your lovely bubble is a splash of water on the floor.

But look at the floor: it all seems to be covered with soft white foam! Maybe it's all our soap suds that are bubbling up around us. Let's try walking over the foam. □ Isn't it strange, the way your foot sinks slowly through the foam until you finally touch the floor? And how high you have to lift the other foot so that it can reach over the top of the foam! Your arms certainly help you to keep your balance. □ Stop where you are. Shut your eyes. □ When you open them again, all the foam will be gone.

End the record. Clap your hands.

Open your eyes. It's all gone! Quickly, each of you take a partner and stand facing each other. □ Find enough space to work together, without touching any other pair of children or the walls. □ Now decide between you who is going to be "A" and who is going to be "B." □

"A," stand up straight with your hands at your sides; "B" is going to trace your outline as you stand there. "B," take your black crayon and, starting at one side of your partner on the floor at his feet, trace a line close to his body without touching him. Go all the way up one side, and around his head. Watch what you are doing and really look at the outline as you do it. □ Now, continue tracing a line all the way down his other side to the floor. □ All finished. Take a long look at your drawing around your partner. □

"B," now take a red crayon, place it on the floor ready for you to start your drawing near the foot of your partner, and shut your eyes. □ "A," watch closely what your partner is going to do, because you do want to have a good outline of yourself when he is finished. Ready, "B." Keeping your eyes shut tight, draw your partner's outline with the red crayon, again without touching him. Draw all the way up one side, around his head, and then back down the other side to the floor. □ When you have finished, open your eyes and check your red drawing; then sit on the floor with your partner. □ Let's talk with the artists who drew the pictures about their work. Which one did you like best? Did you think the black drawing and the red drawing were good outlines? □ Maybe you liked one drawing more than the other, but I think they were both pretty good outlines of your partner!

Now, did any of the "A's" notice any difference in the size of the two drawings? □ Was the red one the same size as the black one? □

Accept all the children's answers, but the one you want is: "The red one was larger than the black one; it had more space between the body and the outline." If the children do not give you this answer, do not supply it for them, since it is always important for the children to discover the answers for themselves. Ask them to think about the answer to the question while they try the next exercise. If they do give the required answer, say:

That's what happened. When our eyes are closed, we draw things larger than they really are.

Whatever answers you received, continue with the next exercise.

Stand up again. This time, "B" stand with his feet apart and his hands on his hips. Get into a good position that you can hold. "A," take a long handled brush, dip it in the blue paint, and, beginning at the side of one foot on the floor, begin to trace your partner's outline all the way around him without touching his body. □ When you have finished, stand back and carefully look at the outline you have made. □ "B," jump and bring your feet together and your arms down to your sides with a slap. Now, jump back into the position you were in when "A" made your outline. □ Good. That looks the same.

Now "A," take your brush again, dip it in the orange paint pot, and put it at the side of your partner's foot ready to begin. □ "B" will have to keep very still if he doesn't want to have orange paint on his clothes, and he had better watch closely where his partner is painting. Ready, artists; shut your eyes and begin to trace the outline of your partner again. When you reach the floor on the other side, open your eyes and think about your drawing. □ Ask yourself if there is any difference in the size of your blue outline and that of the orange one. □ "A," stand facing your

partner in the position you had when your outline was drawn; and "B," hold the position you had when your outline was painted. Both of you, think and talk about the difference between the two outlines you each drew. □

Clap your hands.

Everybody sit on the floor. □ Now we have lots of outlines to talk about. First of all, were the blue outline and the orange one the same size this time? □ Which was the larger? □ When we picture the orange outline, it is almost as though we had on a large space suit. Now think carefully; when you stood facing your partner and looked at the outlines of the positions you each held your body in, was there any difference in their shape? □

Accept all their ways of expressing these differences and continue:

Yes, the way you held your body made a different shape for the outline. Up on your feet and stand facing your partner. □ On the loud drumbeat, see if you can make another different shape for an outline with your body, and then hold that shape.

Make several quick beats, then a loud beat.

What interesting shapes you made! Relax. □ Again on the loud beat, see if you can make *another* different shape.

Use the same drum effect.

Good. Now see if, with your partner, you can together make a shape for an outline.

Use the same drum effect, then continue:

Hold it, and look around at some of the others. □ Isn't it wonderful how many different shapes we can think of to make with our bodies? Now each one of you is a spaceman. Go to your locker where your space suit is hanging, and put it on. □ There are long legs on the suit to get into. Do up all the fasteners that are down the front. □ Now comes the big space helmet. Put it on carefully, so that it rests on your shoulders and you can see where you are going. □ Some of us forgot to put on our big boots! □

Start a record. (A modern, electronic sound. Suggested: the theme from *2001: A Space Odyssey*.)

Now, try walking over the ground to your space ship across the room. □ Are the boots heavy to walk in? What does your big suit feel like? □ Now you have reached your space ship; get in and close the

door. □ Prepare for take-off, and you are away. Look down at the earth as you zoom higher in the sky. What does it look like now? □
We zoom past the stars, and I think the moon is right ahead of us. Wouldn't it be exciting to land on it? Bring your space ship down, and make a soft landing. □ Open the door carefully, and slowly get out of your ship to walk around. □ What does the ground feel like under your feet? How do you feel when you are walking in space? □
We don't want to stay too long. We'd better get back into our ships. □ Close the door and head back to earth. □ We have all landed safely. Get out of your space ship, go to your locker, and take off your suit. □ And report over here to talk about your trip. □

Indicate the place. End the record.

Quickly, see if you can be here by the time I count to ten.

Count one to eight rather quickly, then use the counts of nine and ten to gather up the stragglers.

Did you like being a spaceman? □ What did it feel like when you walked in your boots on the earth? □ Was it fun to be a spaceman and land on the moon? □ Would you like to make up a story about it?
We will say that there are four spacemen in each ship; they prepare for take-off, and then zoom out into space. When at last they land on the moon, at first, only one man goes down the ladder to see what kind of ground it is that covers this part of the moon and whether it is safe to walk on. He reports to the other spacemen in the ship, and then they all go together to explore.
We'll think that they see some large shapes that have been there on the moon all the time. When the spacemen get near to them, the shapes begin to move. What are they? Are they plants or trees, or animals or people? I don't know. I think the shapes will have to decide what they really are. Then the spacemen will have to find this out when they do the story and decide whether to run back to their space ship and return to earth fast, or whether they will try to capture one or two of the shapes and bring them back to earth.
Each group can decide how it wants the story to end.

Dividing the children into two groups as they sit there, continue:

Mary, you will take these children and work over there, and Peter, you will work with this group over here. In each group, quickly choose who you are in the story and where the moon is to be placed. Then decide where you are going to have the space ship land on the moon. You can all have 10 minutes to prepare and do your story. Get to work quickly, and maybe we will have time to see each other's stories.

Walk among the children to observe where they need help to get them under way. Assist them only if necessary. As they get near the end of their drama, say:

One minute to finish up.

After a minute, with a loud clap of the hands, say:

Everyone finish up, and sit down where you are.

If time permits, have each group do their story, sharing their work with the rest of the class. Make no comment on the standard of the work, but do single out any good ideas they have worked out together. Especially mention any good teamwork in the creation of interesting shapes. If there is time only for a discussion, question the children about their experiences. You might say:

What were the shapes in this group? What did you do about them? What kind of ground did you find covering the moon? What did *your* shapes turn out to be? Thank you all for your good thinking.

Note: If you still have time after the discussion, reverse the roles within the groups and have the groups think up another idea to play out.

If you wish, you may carry this theme over to another class. Then, at the beginning of the next class, give the children some warming-up exercises based on this session. Suggest that: they are dandelion heads that have gone to seed, light fluffy balls that are blown by soft breezes: they float and twirl, and finally are all blown apart so that they land on the ground every which way. With groups of two, make interesting shapes and suggest that the shapes move to a slow drumbeat. With groups of four, have the children make large shapes that are plants: the wind, as it blows through them, makes them move their long branches of leaves.

Use a soft slow sound on the drum, which you can build to a climax if you wish. The wind suddenly stops, and the leaves fall back into a position on the plant. Gather the children into a group around you, and talk over the previous session about the landing on the moon. Get them to recall what the groups did, what they saw, and how they worked out their ideas. Divide the children into two groups again, using different leaders from the last time. Allocate each group a space to work in, and have them redo the story. End the lesson as previously, either with a sharing of their work or with a further discussion of their experiences.

NINE

Theme:

SWITZERLAND

Emphasis:

Improving observation

Materials: Drum.
Record.
  SUGGESTED: *A Walk in the Black Forest,* Jankowski.

For the beginning of the lesson, place enough chairs for half your class in a circle, with the seats facing into the centre. Do this yourself or ask the children to help you.

Today, each take a partner, and the two of you stand behind a chair—by the time I beat a loud drumbeat.

Give a loud drumbeat, and proceed:

Good. Now, when the music starts, I want you to walk all around the room and look very carefully at the different things in it. Notice everything you can on the walls, the ceiling, and even the floor. Away you go; help each other to notice everything, but talk quietly.

Start the music. (A lively march. Suggested: *A Walk in the Black Forest,* Jankowski.) Give the children about three or four minutes, then fade the music out.

Come back to the circle. Now, one partner will sit on his chair, and the other partner will stand behind it. □ On the loud drumbeat, everyone freeze.

Make a loud drumbeat.

The children sitting on the chairs are to close their eyes; I am going to ask them questions about what you have seen in the room. It will be your turn to answer when I touch you on the head. Your

partner, who is standing behind you, will tell you whether your answer is correct. So those on the chairs, close your eyes. □ Everyone think hard and try to remember what you saw.

Touch a child gently on the head and leave your hand there.

How many doors are there in this room?

Touch another child.

What color are the doors?

Proceed to touch different children for each question, giving each child who is sitting down at least one turn to answer.

Remember to keep your eyes shut tight, all you children who are sitting down.

Some sample questions are:

Are there any pictures hanging on the walls? What kind of lights are there in this room? Are the drapes a plain material, or do they have a pattern in them? Were any of the windows open? What color are the walls? Did you notice anything special on the walls? What is the floor made of? What color are the chairs? Do the chairs have any metal on them? What part of the chair is metal?

Ask any other questions that are appropriate to your room, but keep the questioning brisk and have it last for only a short time.

Good. Now stand up and, to the drumbeat, run around the circle of chairs with your partner.

Begin to drum with a quick beat, and build to a

climax of a loud beat and say:

Freeze! Look at your partner carefully, and notice all the things you can about his appearance — what he looks like and what he is wearing.

Allow a few minutes for the children to do this.

With your partner, return to your chair. The one who was sitting will now stand up, and his partner will sit on the chair with his eyes closed. □ Keep your eyes shut tight, and this time I will ask you questions about your partner's appearance, and he will tell us whether you are correct.

Touch one child's head.

What kind of dress is your partner wearing?

Touch another.

What color was yours wearing?

Touch another child, and continue as in the previous exercise.

Does your partner have on running shoes? Is yours wearing anything in her hair? How has yours combed his hair? How does your partner keep his shoes on his feet? How are they done up? What color socks is yours wearing? Has yours got a watch on his wrist? Is your partner wearing a sweater? What piece of clothing on your partner is blue? Where does your partner have any buttons that show? How many rings has yours on her fingers? Can you tell me the color of your partner's eyes? Does your partner have curly hair or straight hair? Does your partner have a belt on? Tell me the color and kind of stockings your partner is wearing? Everybody open their eyes. You're very observant; it was hard to trick you. Stand up. □ This time, each child will work by himself. To the music, walk to the school over there.

Indicate the place.

Carefully watch the route you are walking as you go to school.

Start the record. After the children have reached their destination, fade the music down.

You put your hand in your pocket and discover you have lost the ten cents that you brought for the class project. □ Try to remember the way you took to school, and go back to the chairs the same way and look for the dime.

Turn the music up, then watch the children until they each find their coin.

When you find your dime, pick it up and go back to school.

When they reach the school, turn the volume of the music down.

Now this next time, let's say that, to the music, you look everywhere and still can't find the dime. Stop looking for it on the drumbeat, and decide whether you are going back to school without it, or whether you will go home, which is at the chairs. Each one make up his own mind and go to one place or the other. Start to try and find the dime again.

Start the music, and after a few minutes make the drumbeat and pause. Then continue the music until all the children are finished the exercise.

Sit down and relax. Do any of you have pets? What kind do you have? and you?

Encourage the children in a discussion of pets; ask them the names of their pets.

Think of your pet. If you haven't one, think of one you would like to have and what you would call him. Now go to your home anywhere in the room.

Start the record again at a low volume.

It is after school, and you open the front door and call to your pet. □ Listen for him. He doesn't answer. Search for him all over the house. □ Finally, you think where you can find him. □ This time, let us try to see the exact moment when you discover him. □ When you find your pet, sit down and play with him.

When all the children are sitting down, walk around and discuss with them where they found their pets and what kind of pets they have.

Now you can play with your pet for a few minutes.

From your observations of how each child is playing with his pet, phrase a suitable question for him, as:

Wasn't he a big dog to get lost? Where did you find him? That turtle must have been hard to find! What a fluffy kitten! Didn't you hear him meow? Goodness, what kind of an animal is that? Where was that bad boy hiding? Where do you usually keep your guinea pig? How did you ever find that tiny iguana?

Do this for a few minutes, until their attention weakens, and then fade out the record.

Now put all your pets safely away, and let's make two groups.

Divide the class into two.

One group here.

Indicate the chairs.

And the other one over there.

Choose another part of the room with enough space for the children to work. Then speak to the children who are at the chairs.

In this group each child kneel down in front of a chair and drum your fingers on the seat of the chair to make the sound of rain lightly falling. ☐ You do that very well. Now rest for a minute, while I get the other group working.

To the other group, suggest:

Each one of you lives in a house along the street here.

Indicate the place.

Now, go into your house. ☐

To gain everyone's attention, clap your hands.

We'll say that this group of boys and girls can't find their pets anywhere in the house, and they have to go out and try and find them. But today it is raining, and this group will make the sound of rain for us. (Indicate the children by the chairs.)

Begin the rain now, and let's see what happens. Really look hard until you find your pet, and don't forget that it is really wet out.

Give the children time to become involved with the situation.

Two minutes to finish up, and then return home again.

Pause and then make a loud clap for the finish.

That was good work together. Now we'll have the groups quickly change places. ☐ This time, when I tell the rainmakers, it will begin to rain harder. The boys and girls will look everywhere, but they won't find their pets, and they will have to go home for their supper alone. Start the rain falling lightly. ☐ And you other children, begin to search around outside for your pets.

After some work has been done, continue:

Now it is raining harder. ☐ The children are getting soaked, but they look everywhere — under the veranda, up in the tree, behind the garbage tins, and behind the garage. Think of some more places to look.

Pause for a moment, then say:

You can't find your pet, and it is time to go in for your supper.

Pause again, and finally clap your hands to signal the finish of the exercise.

That was nice work done by the rainmakers. I thought it was sad that the boys and girls couldn't find their pets, because they did look very hard for them in all that rain. All come over here and sit down. ☐

Have any of you heard or seen the story of Heidi? Do you know where she lived? ☐ Do any of you know where Switzerland is? ☐ That's right across the ocean in Europe; and do any of you know if there are any mountains in Switzerland? ☐ Oh, yes, it is almost all mountains. What kind of animals do you think eat grass on the mountains? ☐ Yes, sheep, goats, and cows. And who do you suppose looks after the animals? ☐ Well, it is mostly the boys and girls who on summer days lead the animals up the mountain to graze on the nice green grass.

The people live in wooden houses, and they have a fenced in place next to each house where they keep the sheep and the goats at night. In the morning the father works on the land growing hay for the animals to eat in the winter time, and the mother packs a lunch for the children. The children think it is a wonderful adventure to set off up the mountains to look after the animals for the day. It is almost like a picnic; while the animals feed, the children can talk and play around together. Then, when it begins to get dark, they lead their sheep or goats down the mountain again.

Let's think that we are in Switzerland. We will divide up into smaller groups, and then each group can do their own story about a family who lives there. Let's say that there is a mother and father and two children living in each house, and that they have four sheep or goats to look after. The children can help give the animals their names.

Try and make up funny ones, such as Zip and Zock or Tick and Tock. What are some funny names that you can think of?

Listen to a few suggestions from some of the children, then say:

All these are good ideas, but you can decide about the names when you are in your groups. We'll think that the family gets up in the morning, and after breakfast the children set off with the animals, who are really like pets, aren't they? After lunch the children fall asleep. It begins to rain, and the raindrops awaken them. The children look around everywhere, but the animals have gone. Let's have each group decide on an ending for the story. Think of how and where you could find your animals, and how you could take them safely down the mountain to your home.

Divide the class into groups of 8 and give each group a place to build their house. After you do this, clap your hands for their attention.

Decide in each group who will be the father, the mother, the two children, and the animals. Choose what kind of animals they are to be and what their names are. Next, build your house and the place for the animals to sleep, and then begin to do your story. I will clap my hands 10 minutes from now as a warning that it is time for you to finish up your story.

Walk among the groups, guiding them by your questions to iron out their difficulties, and see that everyone is at work as soon as possible. The children will seem to take a long time over the domestic scene of waking up and breakfast, but don't worry; it is familiar ground for them. If you listen to their dialogue and observe their actions, you will discover a great deal of each child's own family life. If one group is finished far ahead of the others, you can ask this group to repeat their story for you. Your interest and questions based on what you have seen them do together could lead these children to think in more detail another time. When the allotted time is nearly up, or if you see most of the groups are finishing, clap your hands and say:

Two minutes to finish.

Pause. Then with two loud claps, say:

Everyone sit down where he is. Wasn't that fun? I saw some wonderful stories. This group, tell us what happened to your sheep when the children were asleep? □ And did you get them home safely? □

Ask another group:

Where were your sheep hiding? □ Did your father come to help you get them down? □ Was your mother glad to see you come back with all the sheep? □ What did you name your goats? □ How many boys and girls were soaking wet when they got back home? □ What did you do with your wet clothes? □

Listen as the children give their answers, and encourage them to talk about their stories.

Good, how would you like to change the parts around in your group? The animals are now the mother and father and children, and the others in each group are the animals.

This time we'll change our story a little. Let's say that, when the animals are grazing, only one of them gets lost. The children decide that one child should stay with the rest of the animals while the other child hunts for the missing pet. During the search, the child falls and breaks his ankle. Now think how you can work this story out together. Do you find the missing sheep or goat? How are you all going to get safely back home again?

Quickly decide what part you are this time, and begin to work on your new story. I will clap my hands in 10 minutes.

Walk among the children while they work. This time you should see them working in greater depth and becoming more involved with details. Always assist them if they seem to be in trouble among themselves, or if they need further directions. After 10 minutes or less, clap your hands.

Two minutes to finish your story.

Pause, and then clap your hands twice.

Finish and sit down. There were a lot of good ideas that you used this time.

Ask questions which will lead them into recounting their adventures. To one group, you might say:

Did you like your story better this time? Why?

Of another group, inquire:

How did you end your story?

To another group suggest:

It was very interesting to see the way you ended your story. Why did you decide on that ending?

Carry on the discussion with the children for as long as time and their interest permit.

Wasn't it wonderful to do your own story? You can do so again another day. Thank you for all your good work.

TEN

Theme:

THE OLD HOUSE

Emphasis:

Improving sense of touch

Materials: Drum.
Records.
  SUGGESTED: *Pictures at an Exhibition*, Moussorgsky.
  Jeux—poème dansé, Debussy.

To begin the lesson, make a loud beat on the drum, and say:

Freeze! This floor is all covered with eggs. When the music starts, try to step on and crack as many eggs as you can.

Start the music. (A sprightly rhythm. Suggested: "Ballet of the Unhatched Chicks," *Pictures at an Exhibition*, Moussorgsky.)

They are all over the place. Don't forget the ones beside you. □ There are quite a few behind your back. □ I still see some that are right in front of you. There are just one or two left. □ Now they are all cracked. Clear away all the mess and come and sit over here.

Fade out the music.

Shut your eyes. Everything is dark. Put your hand up to your cheek, and rub your fingertips gently over your face. Think what it feels like. □ Now, still with your eyes closed, rub your teeth with your finger. □ Do your teeth feel the same as your cheek? What do you think is the difference? □

Clap your hands.

All open your eyes. What did the skin on your face feel like? □ Yes, it felt smooth, soft. Anything else?

Accept other answers, and then ask:

What different feeling did your teeth have when you rubbed them with your fingertips? □ (Hard.) What was the same kind of feeling that you noticed when you touched your teeth and face? □ (Smooth.) Now, with your eyes open, see if you can put your hand on another part of you that would be smooth to the touch. □ Good. I see some of you have touched your other hand, your neck, and, yes, your knees. Could you find something smooth to the touch in anything you are wearing? □ Now could you find a different kind of feel in something that you are wearing? □ When you do, leave your hand there and think how you could tell us in words what it feels like. □ John, what kind of material did you find? □ Yes? □ And you, Mary? □ You are touching your shoe; what does it feel like? □ What kind of feel has your sweater? □ What do you think your buttons feel like? □

Ask a few other children to describe what kind of texture they have found, then say:

Look around the room and see if you can see anything you think would have a smooth touch. □ On the drumbeat, get up and go and touch it, stay there; and really feel it to see if you are right. □

Beat the drum once.

A lot of you did find something smooth to touch: a window pane, the desks, the floor, the seats of the chairs, and even the door. Now, to the drumbeat,

walk around the room and with your fingertips touch as many different kinds of things as you can and try to think what each one feels like.

Beat a slow march on the drum.

On the loud beat freeze where you are, with your hand still touching something you are feeling. □ Freeze.

Make a loud drumbeat. Discuss with the children some of the unusual surfaces. Use as examples: "What do the curtains feel like? The wastepaper basket? The underside (or the legs) of a chair?

Good work. Now relax. How many know what cobwebs look like? Mary, tell us. □ Yes, and you had something to add, John? □ Does anyone know what cobwebs feel like?

Have the children try to describe the feel of cobwebs.

The room is all covered with cobwebs hanging from the ceiling and the walls. They are all over the room. It is quite dark in here.

If possible, turn down the lights.

To the drumbeat, move around and try to clear the cobwebs away from in front of you with your fingertips.

Start a very slow beat, varying it with a few quick ones. After a short while, say:

Freeze. There, the cobwebs are all cleared away now. Now, all go down to that end of the room. □

Indicate which end. Beat the drum once.

Line up facing this way with some room between each one of you. □ To the drumbeat, walk this way: but I am going to make it difficult for you. You must shut your eyes and think about walking on the smooth floor. Ready, all eyes shut.

Start a marching beat in a natural walking rhythm, and then with a loud beat say:

Freeze! Good. Why was it easy to walk on a smooth floor with your eyes shut? □ Yes, you knew the floor was going to be there right under your feet for each step. Now turn around and be ready to walk back to that end of the room with your eyes shut. □ I'll make it still harder for you, because this time you must think that the floor is all covered with large stones. Shut your eyes and try to feel with your foot where you can take each step. Ready?

Begin a slower beat on the drum for their walking

action, and end the exercise with a loud beat.

Freeze! Open your eyes. It was harder, wasn't it? □ When the ground is uneven, you have to feel very carefully with your feet before you take a step, or you might fall down. Everybody run and get a chair, and we'll make a tunnel with the chairs here. □

Indicate the place. Place the chairs in two parallel lines, with the seats facing outward and the backs about two feet apart. The tunnel should be about fifteen feet long. If you have 30 or 40 children, make two tunnels and divide the children into two groups.

Now all line up at the opening of the tunnel. □ This tunnel is made of stones and earth; it is high enough for you to stand up in, but it is dark inside. To make it dark when you enter the tunnel, shut your eyes. Put your hands behind your back and see if you can walk through it without your body touching the sides. When the person ahead of you is part way through the tunnel, you start out. All ready. Begin.

Start a drumbeat of medium rate.

Open your eyes when you think you are at the end of the tunnel, and quickly go back to your place in the line.

When the last child is through the tunnel, make a loud beat and say:

Freeze! Wasn't that fun? A good many of you did reach the end, and there was hardly any bumping into the sides of the tunnel. Now this is a dark, low, secret tunnel through stones and mud that leads into an old empty house. You will have to crawl through it with your eyes shut. Think what it feels like when you touch the floor of the tunnel with your hands and knees. This time we are going to go through to the music. Don't forget to wait until the child ahead of you is part way through before you enter the tunnel. When you get to the end, open your eyes and you will be in one of the rooms of the old house. Walk around and see what it looks like.

Start the record. (Reflective, mysterious music. Suggested: *Jeux—poème dansé*, Debussy.)

Away you go. □

When most of the children are through the tunnel suggest:

What room do you think this is in the house? □

What is that over in the corner? Blow the dust off it; touch it with your hands. □ Look at the dirty windows, I'll bet you could write your name on the glass! □ Look at the old chairs; what are they made of? Try and find out. □

There are a lot of cobwebs in the doorway, clear them aside and go into the hall. □ There's a stairway. Put your hand on the railing; I wonder what it is made of? □ Go upstairs carefully; one of the stairs may be missing. □ Look at all the rooms. I wonder if any children lived here? □

Let's go into that little room at the end of the hall. □ Put your hand on the knob of the door, it feels very old and rusty. □ I wonder if the door squeaks? Open it, a little at a time. □ Look, there is a little bed, and over there a toy chest — at least I think it is. Go and find out. □ Feel around the top for the lock. □ You found it; now open the box and see what it has inside. □ Take out one of the toys and examine it. □ It may be old, but it is very nice. It doesn't seem to belong to anyone now. I wonder what the child was like. Better put it back in the box and close the lid. □

It seems to be getting darker now. Go to the window and put your hands on the window sill to look out. □ What a long way down! □ It's getting late. Let's go down the same stairs again; careful of that step. □ Look, there's the front door, but it's a heavy one. Use both hands and pull hard; see if you can open it. □ You did! Shut it again, and run back home over here before it is dark. □

Fade out the music. Discuss their adventure with the children and emphasize their sense of touch. The following are some suggested questions. "When you were going upstairs was there a step missing?" "What did you think the railing on the stairs felt like?" "What was it made of?" "Did you find a toy in the toy chest?" "What was it?" "What was it made of?" "Was it a big toy, or could you hold it in your hand?" "Who do you think played with the toy you found?" "How do you know it was a very little girl or boy?" "Where did you find the lock on the chest?" "How did you find the lock?" "What do you think the chest was made of?" "Why?" "Were there any old chairs in the first room you were in?" "What do you think they were made of?"

"Did they have any material on them?" "What did the material feel like?" "When you blew the dust off the object in the corner, what was it?" "What did it feel like?" "Was the window smooth when you wrote your name on it?" "When you were in the tunnel on your hands and knees, what did the ground feel like?" "Did you think it felt dry and warm?"

The following questions are important to ask as an introduction to the next section. "When you think of an old empty house, what do you imagine it looks like from the outside?" "What is your old house made of?" "Yes, and you Mary?" "Anyone else?" "Does it have a front porch on it?" "Was the porch falling apart?" "What was it made of?" When this discussion starts to wane, say:

Do you think it would be fun sometime on a holiday to go and explore an old house? Of course, you wouldn't have to go alone. I know of some boys and girls who one day went together to explore an old house, and they had an exciting adventure. Let's think of a story we could do about an adventure in an old house. Shall we start with some children who find themselves near an old house? Why are they there? □

Accept various answers and choose one, such as that the children are on a picnic or a hike. Then continue:

The children become curious about the old house. They walk around it and finally decide to go in. Do you think they can open the front door? □ Yes, let's say they can. It takes a lot of effort, but they do manage to open it. Now there are lots of things that could happen once they are inside. What are some ideas?

Listen to the children's ideas.

There are so many ideas, maybe we should leave that part of the story for each group to choose the idea that it wants to use. Then, to continue our story, let's say that the children go down into the cellar to search for an old treasure. They find it; and just after they have decided to take it up the stairs, the wind blows the cellar door tight shut. The children can't open the door, there are no windows in the cellar, and it is so dark they have to feel their way around. How do you think they could find a way out of the cellar?

You will probably get the answer of "a tunnel" from one of the children.

Yes, I think a tunnel is about the only way out, don't you? How do you think they find the tunnel?

Listen to their ideas and then repeat them, urging the children to enlarge on their suggestions. The following is an example of how to lead the children to explore their own ideas: "They could be sitting on a stone; how would they find it was loose? Would it be easy to move? Would the tunnel be big enough for them to crawl through?" When the children have considered various escape methods, ask all the next four questions together without waiting for an answer:

When the children get out at the other end of the tunnel, where are they? Is it near their home? Did they bring the treasure with them? What do they do with it? There could be so many different ideas from these questions. Suppose in each group you think of the end of the story among yourselves. Maybe if we work well, we will have time to see each other's adventure today.

Divide the children into groups of eight and allocate a place for each group to work. This time, go over to the groups in turn and appoint a leader for them. To one group you might say:

Mary is going to be the leader of your group today, to help you sort out your ideas so that you can get down to work quickly. You will have ten minutes to do your story.

Make sure each group has enough chairs or other equipment to build a house and a tunnel. If a group needs help to get started, ask them questions that will spur them on, such as: "Where is the front door?" "Which area have you set aside for the cellar?" "How are you going to make the tunnel?" "Which children are going to make it?" "Where is

the treasure going to be?" "Have you decided what the treasure is?" When the action is under way, leave it to the children to work the story out themselves, and just observe their work. At the end of the allotted time, clap your hands.

Two minutes to finish up.

Make a loud beat on the drum.

Freeze! □ Let's ask this group to share their adventure first, and the rest of us will sit down over here.

Indicate the place and sit with the children.

We are all ready for you to start.

At the close of the drama, the group will probably say "That is all." If they don't indicate the end, when you think they have finished, say:

Thank you. It was very good the way you . . . .

Make some comment on one part of the work that you can honestly say they have done well together.

Now let's sit over here where the other group were working, and we will see what they have done together. □ We are all quiet; now you can begin.

Again at the close of the drama, thank them and make an honest comment on their teamwork, or on the playing out of a good idea. Then to all the class say:

All sit down for a minute. Did you all enjoy your adventure? □ What part did you enjoy most? □ Were you glad when you found the entrance to the tunnel? □ Was it nice to be out in the open again? □ You have done some very good work together today.

Special Note: Do not ask the children who are watching the drama to comment out loud on the work they have seen. They will be able to make a silent comparison for themselves. Ignore any criticism of another person's work that you may hear during the last discussion. The aim is for each child to learn to assess his own work for himself.

ELEVEN

Theme:

THE TOYMAKER

Emphasis:

Developing concentration

Materials: Drum.
Record.
SUGGESTED: *The Nutcracker,* Tchaikovsky.

Ask the children all to come over to you. When they have arrived, give a loud beat on the drum, and say:
Freeze! You are all given permission to go to the shopping plaza over there across the street.
Indicate a place in the classroom.
You can go this afternoon to see all the beautiful toys that are on show in the windows.
Start the record. (Suggested: excerpts from *The Nutcracker.*)
Away you go. Be careful crossing the road. □ Now you are there. In the window of the shop in front of you, there are a great many mechanical toys. Look at them all. □ What do you suppose makes the robot blink his eyes? □ How does that steam shovel scoop up and lift the stones? □ Do you think the walky-talky set would really work? □ Do you see anything else interesting? □
In the next store there are some trains going around in the window. Which kind of train do you like best? □ Which one do you think goes the fastest? □ How many bridges over the river can you count? □ Boy, look at those signals! I wonder what makes them work. □
Oh, your sister wants you to go with her to look at the dolls. □ There they are. □ I wonder what she sees in those big walking dolls. □ Can they really talk? □ The Barbie dolls are quite small, but look at all the clothes they have! □ There are some others dressed in different costumes; I wonder what country they are from? □ Up there at the back is a big soldier doll. Wow, just look at his uniform! □ Look in the window of the next store; they have all different kinds of toys. Do you like the jack-in-the-box? □ It's neat the way he goes up and down. Look how high he jumps up! What a lot of things to see— stuffed animals, meccano sets! There sure are a lot of toys! □
You put your hand in your pocket and find that you have some real gold coins. □ You can go into any store you want to and buy the toy that you like the best. □ Quickly go in and buy it, then bring it back home here. □
Indicate the place.
Sit down and play with your new toy. □
Fade out the music and make a loud beat on the drum.
Freeze! Take a partner sitting near you, and each tell the other all about the toy you have bought, and explain how it works. □ Freeze! Let's all share the interesting toys that you bought.
Discuss the toys with the children. From your observations, make such suggestions as:
Mary, tell us all about your doll. □ John, how does your partner's mechanical toy work? □ Jane, in

what is Barbara's doll dressed? □ Susan, what kind of train did Peter buy? □ Billy, what was the big toy you brought home? □ What do you do with yours, Sarah?

Continue to ask interesting questions about the toys. When the children's attention begins to wane, continue:

Let's put all the toys carefully on the floor at the sides of the room and quickly find a space to work in the centre. □ Good. See that there is lots of room around each one of you. Now sit on the floor. □ Do you remember the jack-in-the-box? He is all curled up tight in his box, and when the lid is opened, he springs up. You are all jack-in-the-boxes. Crouch down as low as you can, and hold your arms tightly around your knees. □ Listen to the drum, because on the loud beat the lid of your box is going to open and you will spring out. Ready.

Start soft quick beats on the drum, leading up to a sharp bang.

Let's try it again. First of all be tightly crouched in your box, and then really spring up. □ Ready, and listen.

Produce the same rhythm on the drum.

That was fun! Some of you sprang up so high that you fell over. All sit down for a minute. □ Quietly listen to the music that I'm going to play for you, and think about what kind of dolls you can see moving around or dancing to it.

Use a very short extract from the second act of *The Nutcracker* to suggest a mechanical doll. Fade out the record and continue:

What kind did you see? □ Yes, and you? □

The children should give you the answer of a mechanical kind of doll, robots, wooden soldiers, walking dolls, etc. At the end of this discussion, start to play the waltz section of the same record, which should create for the children the image of dancing dolls. After a short time, stop the record, and ask the children:

What kind of doll did you see that time? □ Yes, ballerinas, skating dolls, dancing dolls. Did any of you see the boy dolls that looked like princes running and leaping up in the air so lightly they seemed to float? □ You did. They were wonderful to watch. Now think what other kind of doll you can see dancing to this music.

Start the record at the section made up of dances from various countries. After a short time, stop the record.

There were a lot of different dolls dancing that time, all dressed in lovely costumes. What were some of them? □ Russian. Can anybody guess what kind of boots he would be wearing? □ Yes, big black ones. Some of you said Scandinavian.

Pick out some of the nationalities suggested by the children. Be sure to mention, also, dolls from Poland, Hungary, Czechoslovakia, or any other country from which some of the children or their families may have emigrated.

Did the girl dolls have any ribbons in their hair? □ What kind of ribbons were they? □ What were their dresses like? □ Were there any boy dolls from these countries? □ Does anybody know what their costumes were like? □

If the children do not know, suggest to them that you have seen some handsome ones with black pants and little jackets. They had on white shirts with big sleeves, and around their waists the boys wore belts of many bright colors, such as red, green, blue, and gold.

I will play that music again, and you are all dolls, from whichever country you like, who will dance to it. Think of the costume you are wearing. Listen to the music, and you can dance the way it tells you to. □

Start the record again at the same place.

What a lot of colorful dolls you are! Dance anywhere in the room you want to. □

When they are physically tired, suggest:

Now you are all rag dolls. □ And you dance so fast you fall in a heap on the floor.

Stop the record. Then clap your hands.

Do you remember this music?

Start the record at the section you used for the mechanical doll. □

Stand up. □ You are all robot dolls walking around. Think that you are all made of metal and your insides are all nuts and bolts. □ You must be well oiled; I can't hear one creak in any of your joints.

After a few minutes, lower the volume for the

following suggestion and the children's replies.
Maybe some of you could think of another doll that the music suggests to you. □

Use one of the suggestions given to you by the children, either vocally or by their change of actions, to offer them another image for this exercise. You might say:

Good. You are all walking dolls. (Raise the volume of the music again.) Move very easily and smoothly, or you might break the motor inside you. □

To finish this section suggest:

Now let's change again. You are all wooden soldiers. You will have to keep very straight because you are made of wood. □ Are you carrying a gun? What color coat do you have with all the shiny buttons on it? How tall is your hat? Does it have a feather on it? □ Now march to your box, get in it, and lie down. □ And the lid closes. □

End the record and, with a loud clap of your hands, continue:

Sit up. I release you all from your enchantment; you are all boys and girls again. Listen to this part of the music again for a minute, and think about the dolls that you can see dancing to it.

Start the record softly at the waltz section, then raise the volume as the children begin to dance.

Now stand up and begin to move or dance around, either as yourself or as any doll that the music suggests to you. You may do any movement that the music makes you want to do. □ Good. Think of as many different movements as you can for your whole body, your arms, your legs, your head, your shoulders, and your waists. □ What lovely dancers you are! All of you are doing such interesting movements to the music. □ Now see if you can end your dance and sit on the floor in time to the music. □

When all the children are sitting, gradually fade out the music.

Very well done. Now as quietly as you can, come over here. □ Dolls are mostly made in a toy factory now, but does anyone know how they used to make dolls a long time ago, before we had big factories? □ If you don't know, perhaps you can guess. □

Listen in turn to the answers from the children. Then continue:

Yes, I think dolls were made by people who formed them with their hands. What do you think a person who made toys was called? □ That would be a good name, "The Toymaker"! In the town, he had a little store where he used to make the toys. We make toys out of all sorts of different materials today, but what material do you think the toymaker used when he carved out the dolls?

Accept the obvious answer, "wood," and continue:

That's right, he used to carve his dolls out of wood, then paint their faces and dress them in different costumes. You all are toymakers. When I clap my hands, you are each going to go to your own little store where you have your wood, tools, paint, and all the different things you need to make a wooden soldier doll for one of the children in the town.

Clap your hands.

Away you go to your store to start your work.

Fade in the record (Suggested: another section from Act II of *The Nutcracker*.) Use it for background music during this entire exercise to help the children concentrate. It will be a delight to see each child so busy in the land of his imagination. When you see that they have become involved with their projects, walk around and speak softly with various children in turn about their wooden soldiers, being careful not to disturb the other children. You could say:

He is handsome. What color coat are you going to put on him? What a brave looking soldier. Is he going to carry a wooden gun? I like the way you painted his eyes; what color hair will he have? Have you made any boots for him yet? What color stripe are you going to put on your soldier's pants, or will he not have any stripes at all? How ever did you polish all those buttons to make them shine so! Why did you choose that lovely color for his coat? How will you make his hat stay on? Did you find a feather for his hat?

When all the children seem nearly finished, say to the class as a whole:

I think the children will be very pleased with all the soldiers. Put the last finishing touches to your own soldier, then have a last look at your work. □ He is nice! Put him safely in a box, shut the lid, and place the box on the shelf. □ What a lot of work you have done today! Clean up the mess and put your tools away. □ Now it is time to leave your store. Don't forget to lock the front door! □ And come home here.

Indicate the place and fade out the record.

You were all such clever toymakers, I am going to tell you a story about another toymaker. Then, all playing together, we'll do the story about him. This toymaker lived in a small village, and his store used to be the favorite one for all the children who lived there. The girls and boys would call for their friends at their homes, and then together they would run down to the toymaker's store to look in the window to see all the wonderful new dolls he had made. Each day there was another different one. What kind of dolls do you think the boys and girls saw? □ I am sure there were all of those: . . . .

Mention those ideas suggested by the children:
wooden soldiers, ballerinas, walking dolls, and Russian dolls.

One day in the window there was the most beautiful doll, who could turn around and dance on her stand. The children could not take their eyes away from her as she twirled around and around, and then suddenly she stopped. They wondered what the toymaker had put inside her to make her dance. Can you guess? □ Yes, I think it was some sort of spring that you could wind up.

That day the children were so busy looking at the new dancing doll, they didn't see the toymaker leave for his lunch. When the doll had stopped dancing for a long while, they ran to the door and they found the store was open. The toymaker had forgotten to lock the door!

When the children ran inside, they didn't see the toymaker anywhere around to ask him to wind up the doll for them again. What do you think they did? □ That's exactly what they did. They took the doll out of the window, and when they discovered she had a key in her back that they could wind up, the girls and boys took turns winding her up and made her dance and dance, until one of the children wound her up too tightly and she was broken! Then some of the children took other dolls out of the window and out of their boxes to play with them, and soon the store was full of dolls and children.

They were so busy playing with the dolls, do you suppose they saw the toymaker coming back from his lunch? □ No, they didn't. He was right in the store before they saw him, and he looked very angry at the mess in his store. Quickly they all tried to hide and run away, but the toymaker caught one of the boys, and he held him so that he could not get away. Then the toymaker put the boy in a chair and tied him up tightly. All the children were quite frightened.

The toymaker began to pick up the dolls and put them away. And that is when he found that his beautiful dancing doll had been broken. He was very sad because she had seemed to be a real live dancer to him. Then he had an idea! If he could make a doll seem to be alive, maybe he could make a real child into a doll. Yes, that is what he would try to do, and he would start that very day with the one naughty boy he had caught.

When the children heard this, because they knew that they were really all to blame for the broken doll and the mess that had been made of the toymaker's store, they gathered together to think of a way to save their friend. Can you think of any plan that the children might have made to help them out of their trouble?

Listen to the plans offered by the children. From these adopt for the ending of the story the plan that seems to meet with the most agreement among the children. Remember the other ideas in case you have time to do the drama more than once. If there aren't any good workable ideas, offer them one of the following:

A. The children offer to the toymaker their allowances, or any money they have saved or been given, to pay for the doll, and they promise never to be so naughty again. The toymaker accepts the money. He thinks he can fix the doll and make her as good as new, and so he lets their friend go free.

B. The children promise the toymaker that they will all help to clean up the store and put everything back in its place, while the toymaker fixes the dancing doll. When the store is all tidy and the doll is fixed, the toymaker lets the boy go home with the rest of the children.

C. The children bring him a magic drink to make him sleep, and while he is asleep they untie their friend and together they all clean up the store. One of the boys is able to fix the dancing doll. She starts to dance again, the toymaker wakes up and is surprised and pleased. He sees all the work the children have done and thanks them. When it is time for the children to go home, he tells their friend to go with them and everybody is very happy.

When you have outlined the chosen plan for the ending, say:

Let's divide up into two groups and do the story of the toymaker now.

Divide the children into two groups.

This group are the children, and they can build their houses over there. □ The other group are the dolls and the toymaker. John, you are our toymaker this time; and Mary, you are the dancing doll.

Choose a boy and a girl who you think will enjoy doing these roles and who have enough self-confidence to be able to do them well.

Each of you in the group is whichever kind of doll you like best. We'll have the store over here.

Indicate the place.

The dolls can all help make the window for us. Everybody start to work and quickly build your places.

You may have to help them share out the equipment. When they have nearly finished their buildings, say to the children:

Let's say that it is night time and everyone is asleep at the beginning of the story. Do you think you would like to have some music when the doll dances? □ All right. That will be my job when the time comes. Everyone take his place and be asleep. □ Now it is morning, and first of all the toymaker wakes up and goes to his store. □ Then all the children wake up and get dressed. □ We will continue with Peter going to each house to call for his friends.

Let the children proceed with the story in their own way. Help only with a suggestion such as, "What happened then?" if they get stuck. Introduce the waltz music when needed, but always keep it as a background to the dialogue of the children. At the finish of the drama, tell the children you liked their work very much, and that they did it well together. Ask them if they would like to do it again. If so, switch the groups and choose other people for the roles of the toymaker and dancing doll. Perhaps, if they seem to have played out the first version, you could use another ending for the drama from one of the alternatives. If they want to stick to the original ending, by all means let them. When you have made these decisions with the children, begin the drama again.

Everybody find his place and quickly shut your eyes, for it is nighttime. □ Now it is morning. First the toymaker wakes up. □ Then the children wake up. □ And Helen will be the child that starts to call on all the boys and girls.

Use the music when necessary during the drama. At the close, again thank the children for all their good work.

Theme:

THE PRINCESS AND THE FROG

Emphasis:

Improving social behavior of children

Materials: Drum.
Records.
SUGGESTED: *The Swan*, Saint-Saëns.
OR: *Greensleeves*, Vaughan Williams.
ALSO: *Rhapsody on a Theme of Paganini*,
Rachmaninoff.

Begin the lesson with a loud beat on the drum,
saying:

Freeze! Half of you go to that end of the room and
line up, and the other half line up at this end of the
room. □ Right. In a moment the two groups are
going to change ends, and each one of you has a
large ball that you are going to bounce as you run
toward the other end of the room. Listen for the
drumbeat and try to bounce the ball on the beat
each time. When you get to the centre of the room
and meet each other, see if you can still keep
control of your ball as you pass. All ready? Begin.
Use a fast steady beat for this action. When most of
the children have reached the ends of the room,
make a loud beat.

Freeze! Good. Not too many people bumped into
each other when they passed. Try the same thing
again, and watch where you are going. As you pass
people from the other group in the centre, see if you
can dodge around each other and still keep your
eye on the ball you are bouncing. Ready. All begin.
Repeat the same drumbeat.

Freeze! Good work. Now throw away your ball and,
at each end of the room, form yourselves into a
straight line. □ Beginning at this side of each end
(Indicate the side.), one at a time each raise a hand
to find out who is standing opposite you in the
other line. He - or she - will then be your partner. □
Make sure the children are paired off.

This time on the drumbeats walk toward your
partner. When you meet in the centre, shake hands
and say, "How do you do" to each other. Begin
walking.
Start the drum with a marching tempo, and end it
with a loud beat when the children meet.

Freeze! That was very well done. Standing with
your partner, turn around and put your backs
together. You are each going to begin walking in
the direction that you are now facing. All listen to
the drumbeats and stop walking one step after the
loud beat. Start walking.
Give a steady marching beat for about eight counts,
then make one loud beat.

And freeze! Do you all know which is your right
hand? □ Good, everybody make a quarter turn to
the right. □ To the drumbeats, continue walking in
the direction that you are now facing.
Begin the same beat again. After five or six times
make a loud beat.

And freeze. Turn and face any other direction you
want. □ You are each going to walk along a straight

line in the direction that you have chosen. But if you bump into another person, you must stop and say, "Excuse me." Then take one step to the side and continue walking until you hear the loud beat. Away you go.

Start beating a walking rhythm, and continue it for at least twelve counts. Then end with a loud beat, and say:

Freeze! How many of you bumped into each other? □ Did you remember to say, "Excuse me"? □ Don't forget that, because we should always say these words when we accidentally bump into another person. While you are standing still, look around the room and see where your partner is. □ Stay where you are and turn to face her or him. □ This time to the drumbeats, you can hop, skip, or jump along the straight line in the direction that you are facing. You are trying to meet your partner; but we are going to make it hard, because every time the loud beat comes you have to stop and make a turn to face in another direction. And what do you say if you cross another person's line and you bump into each other? □ "Excuse me." Then take one step to the side and continue on your way towards your partner. Think what you are doing, and away you go.

Start a quicker beat on the drum and vary it with loud beats. After each loud beat, wait for the children to turn before you begin drumming again. There will be much hilarity, but they are practising a good habit. After a short while, say:

If you and your partner are able to meet, sit down and have a little visit with each other.

When most of the children have reached their partners, give a loud beat and say:

Freeze! This last time, those children who are still standing run to where your partner is and, as you go, dodge all the people that are in your way.

After several very fast beats, end with a loud beat, and proceed:

Everybody sit down and relax for a minute. □ How many of you have seen a real castle? □ Maybe you have a picture in your mind of a favorite one that you have seen on television or in a book. □ What was it like? □

Have the children share their ideas of a castle.

Phrase your questions to the children so that they consider what size and color it is, what kinds of material it might be made of, what the doors are made of, and how the windows and top of the castle are built.

Would it have any water around it; would it have a bridge over the water?

You have so many good ideas, I think we will paint some pictures of castles. Each one of you, use for your canvas a large area beside you on the floor. You have all the colors of paint you will need. Pick up your brush and make a picture of the beautiful castle that you can see in your mind.

Use a record (A graceful, flowing rhythm. Suggested: The Swan, Saint-Saëns, or Greensleeves, Vaughan Williams) as background music for the children to concentrate on their drawing. □ After they have begun to work, walk around and quietly ask one or two of them about their castles. Ask especially those children who you feel need individual help to stimulate their imaginations. Tell them how much you like their drawing, and make inquiries such as: "What color are you going to use for the roof?" "What kind of windows are you going to have?" "When the sun shines on the windows, what color does it make them?" "Is that the front door in the middle?" "What do you think the door is made of?" "What kind of stone is your castle made of?" "What color is it?" To all the class say:

When you have finished your work, put away your brushes and stand up and look at your picture. □ What a wonderful castle! What do they call the people who live in castles like these?

Listen to the children's ideas. Select an answer that has to do with royalty and continue:

Yes, the people in a castle might be a king and queen and their family. And what kind of clothes would they wear?

Listen to the children's descriptions of regal dress. If they haven't mentioned crowns, inquire:

What do kings and queens wear on their heads? □ All the girls are queens. Dress yourselves in your prettiest dresses. Then each take your golden crown and place it on your head. □ Now come and form a circle in the centre. □ And all the boys are kings. Put on your long capes and jewelled golden crowns. □

Now come and stand in a circle around the queens. □ All the queens hold up their right hand. □ Good. Turn to your right and stand facing that way. □ Drop your hands. All the kings hold up their left hands. □ You turn to your left and stand facing in that direction. □ Drop your hands. Now we are going to play a game like musical chairs, only it is called musical people. Because people should always speak to each other nicely when they meet, each time the music stops, you are going to turn to face the person who is opposite you and greet him. Let's try it.

Start the record, and stop it after a moment or so.

I couldn't hear what many of you were saying. What could you say to greet someone when you meet?

Now, in the children's expressions, you will hear something of the child's social training in his home. Mention some of these expressions, if they are socially acceptable, as you continue. For example:

Sometimes we do say "Hello," and if you know the person's name it is friendly to use it too. Then, "How do you do" is fine when you are meeting a person for the first time. It is always polite for people meeting to say "Good morning," "Good afternoon," and "Good evening" to each other. Now that you know many ways in which you can greet each other, the queens turn to their right and the kings to their left. Don't forget to walk to the music with your heads up, or your crowns may fall off. Each time the music stops, turn and face the person opposite you. The king will speak first and greet the queen. Then the queen must speak to the king with the same words of greeting that he used. Start walking.

Start and stop the record several times.

How politely you spoke to each other. Now we'll have the queens turn in the opposite direction, that is, to their left, and the kings turn to their right. This time when the music stops, it will be the queens who will speak first to the kings, and the kings must answer using the same kind of greeting. Ready.

Start the record, and again stop it three or four times.

Hardly anyone missed his turn. They were all friendly greetings that you remembered to say to each other. Now, for this next part, you are all the children of the kings and queens, the lovely princesses and the handsome princes.

Start a lively record for use as a background. (Suggested: Rhapsody on a Theme of Paganini, Rachmaninoff.)

Go out into the garden of the palace and play some games. Play whatever you like. □ I see some of you are playing. . . . □

To stimulate the children's actions, mention some of the games the children have started to play. You might suggest:

Over there, some of you are having a nice walk looking at the flowers. Do any of you have a pet that you would like to play with? Perhaps some of you would like to play at having a tea-party; or perhaps you might play skipping. Some of the princes might like to build a fort. Or how about having a ride on your pony?

Let the children pursue their activities for three or four minutes. At the end of their play, say:

It is time to come back into the palace and sit over here. □

Indicate the place, and fade out the music.

You had a lot of fun playing with each other in the palace garden. I am going to tell you a story about a little princess who had no friends to play with in her palace garden. The princess was the only child of the king and queen. She did her lessons in the morning. Then, after she had her lunch with her mother and father, she would go out into the garden to play.

One day at lunch her father gave her a beautiful golden ball for a present. How happy she was! She thanked the king, and asked if she could take the ball out into the garden. Her mother and father said she could, and she ran out to play.

It was such fun to have something new to play with. She threw the ball up in the air and caught it several times. When she became tired of doing that, she rolled it along the ground.

The princess was enjoying playing with the golden ball so much, she didn't see how close to the deep pool she had come. Then, when she threw it up again, what awful thing do you think happened? □ Yes, it dropped down into the deep pool. The poor little princess sat down by the pool and was very sad that she had lost her new ball.

She was sitting there when she saw an ugly frog hop near her. The princess was so cross at herself, she almost stepped on the poor frog. But the frog croaked and said, "If you will promise me three things, I will get your golden ball from the pond for you." The princess wanted to have her ball back so much that she was willing to promise anything. The frog told her the three things.

If any of the children recognize the story, and they will surely tell you if they do, ask them if they can remember the three things. Then repeat them as you continue with:

First, you will take me into the palace. Second, you will let me sit beside you and eat off your golden plate. And third, you will let me sleep in your own room. The princess promised to do all these things. The frog dived down to the bottom of the pool and brought up the golden ball and laid it at her feet. The princess was so happy to have her ball back; she picked it up and began to run toward the palace. The frog followed her, and with some very loud croaks he called out, "What about your promise?" The princess thought she didn't have to keep her promise, because he was just an ugly old frog, and so she ran on into the palace and closed the door. Soon it was dinner time. The queen, the king, and the princess were having their dinner when there came a knock at the big door. The princess went to the door, and when she opened it, who do you think was there? ▢ It was the frog! It had taken him a long time to get there; he was such a little creature that he couldn't move fast. When he asked the princess to let him in, she didn't want to, and so she closed the door in his face. It was a very rude thing to do. The princess went back to the table, and her father asked her who was at the door. The princess was naughty and said it was nobody. Then there was another knock at the door. This time it was a louder knock. The king said that he would see who was there. When he opened the door, the frog croaked and told the king what the princess had promised him before he brought her ball from the pool. The king told the frog that, if the princess had made a promise, then she must keep it, and he let

the frog come in through the door. The princess was cross when she found out that her father had allowed the frog to come in, but her father said, "A promise is a promise."

The frog came over to the table, and what did he want to do next? ▢ That was it; he wanted to sit next to the princess and eat off her golden plate. Do you think that the princess wanted him to do that? ▢ Not very much, but what did her father say? ▢ "A promise is a promise." So the princess had to have the frog sit beside her and eat off her golden plate. As soon as the dinner was finished, the queen told her daughter it was time for bed. The princess said good night to her parents and started for her room. What do you think the frog wanted to do? ▢ Yes, he wanted to go with her and sleep in her room. The princess was tired of the old frog and didn't want to take him to her room, but what did her father say? ▢ "A promise is a promise." So she had to take him with her.

The frog slept all night in her room. In the morning, when the princess woke up, what a lovely surprise she saw! Instead of the ugly old frog there was a handsome young prince. The prince told her that a witch had cast a spell over him, and when the princess had kept her promises and had been kind to him, the spell had been broken. Now they could play together all the time in the palace garden. The princess was very happy to have a friend. Everyday, now, she always keeps her promises because she remembers — what? A promise is a promise.

Today we will have four people in each group: the king, the queen, the princess, and the frog to do the story. In each group try to decide among yourselves which one of these four parts each person is to take in the story. Quickly get into groups of four and choose a place for your palace.

Assist the children to sort themselves into groups of four and choose a place for their working area. Also, help them to share fairly among the groups the available equipment of tables, chairs, etc. so that each group has sufficient material to build their "palace."

Now get to work making your palaces, and when they are finished start your story. You will have ten minutes to do your story.

When the children are into their dramas, walk around and observe their work. It should be delightful to watch. When they seem to be at the end of their stories, warn them with:

A minute to finish up. □
Clap your hands.

Everyone finish and sit down.
If there was a very good example of teamwork in the doing of the story, ask that group to share their story with the class. Thank them when it is ended, and say how much you enjoyed the good teamwork. If there is enough time, ask the children if they would like to change their parts within their groups and do the story again. If time has run out, thank all the children for their many interesting ways of doing the story.

THIRTEEN

Theme:

NELSON, THE BOY SAILOR

Emphasis:

Developing self-control

Materials: Drum.
Records.
  SUGGESTED: *Ride of the Valkyries*, Wagner.
            La Mer, Debussy.

Before the lesson starts, set about 24 chairs in the outline of a boat with the seats facing toward the inside. Allow a large area for deck space and leave one opening in the perimeter of the chairs for the gangplank. When the children enter the class, have them walk around and try to guess what surprise you have built for them. After a minute or two of this action, make a loud bang on the drum and say:

Freeze! Did anyone guess? □

If the children can't guess, don't be discouraged at your shipbuilding effort. A hint may help them:

Can you think what it might be if it was near, or on, some water? □ A boat! Right!

Have a discussion on boats. Some example questions you might like to use are: "What kind of boats have you been on?" "Sailboats?" "Has anyone ever crossed the ocean in a big boat?" "What was it like?" Then continue:

How many of you have ever seen a picture of a big sailing ship like they used in the olden days? □ What a lot of you have! Let's play a game. Lie down on the floor and shut your eyes. □ Now try to see a picture of a ship of that kind. Think of all you know about sailing ships. I will walk around and touch you on the forehead, then ask you a question about

your sailing ship. □ Ready. All listen carefully, because you never know when it will be your turn to answer.

What is the deck of your ship made of? What are the sails made of? What are they like? What makes sailing ships different from the ships used today on the rivers and oceans? What were sailing ships made of? What did the sailors use to pull up the sails? Did it take a long time to cross the ocean? What did they use to steer the ship? What work did the sailors have to do on the ship? What other jobs can you think of? □ Now open your eyes. Today we are going to be our ship's crew. Stand up. □ You are all sailors. Go on board our sailing ship. Use the opening at the side to walk onto the ship's deck. □ To the drumbeat quickly form a line around the deck of the ship and stand at attention for inspection. □ Be sure to be in place in the line before the drumbeats stop.

Use a quick rolling beat on the drum while they are getting in line, and as soon as all the children are in place, stop beating the drum with a loud bang.

Now salute!

Beat the drum once.

Good. Let's salute again, and try, to a drumbeat, to do it all at the same time.

Make a drumbeat.

Good. Much better. Now take a step to the side with your left foot and put your hands behind your back and stand there "at ease." □ Does anyone know what kind of suit you would be wearing? □ What colour? □ Do you have a hat? □ What do you wear on your feet? □ Why? □

Start the music. (Majestic music, frequently building to climaxes. Suggested: *Ride of the Valkyries*, Wagner.)

To the music, quickly start your training. First of all get a mop and pail and clean the decks. □ They all look nice and clean. Put the pails away, and then climb up the ropes to the lookout at the top of the mast. □ Careful, one hand at a time. Don't lose your footing or you might slip, and it is a long way to fall down. □ There, you have reached the top. Now climb into the lookout, take your telescope, and look out to sea. □ Is there another ship out there? How close is it? Maybe you can see land ahead. How far do you think it is? □ Very good. Now put the telescope back in its place and climb down the ropes again. □

Run to the captain's bridge at the front of the ship and give him your report on what you have seen. □ He lets you steer the ship for a short while. □ Think of the big boat you are steering. How far you have to turn the wheel! Isn't it a large wheel? □

What other duties do sailors have? Of course, peel potatoes. Peel lots and lots of them; all the crew eat so much when they work so hard. □ All done. Take them to the cook. □ Aren't they heavy to carry? □ Now you have to help pull up the ropes for the sails. Pull, pull. The sails are hard to pull up. Pull, pull hard. There they go. They are almost to the top now. The wind catches the sails, and they blow out. Tie the end of the rope around a metal pipe so that the sails will stay blowing in the wind, and the ship can sail faster. □

Suddenly the wind gets stronger and there are a few drops of rain. Then there is more and more rain, and a storm blows up. Waves come crashing over the side, the decks are all wet, and with the strong wind it is difficult to walk. Try and make your way safely to the door of your cabin. □ Isn't it hard to walk there with all the rain and the wind in your face? □ There it is, just ahead. Push the door open. □ Good! Shut the door; inside it's dry. That's it, take off your wet boots and coat. □ Lie in your

bunk for a while and listen to the roar of the sea. □ The storm is over, and now it's time to prepare for landing. Go up on deck and find one of the coils of rope. □ Begin to unwind it. You will need more rope than that to throw onto the dock to hold this big ship. That's better, now throw the rope over the water to the land. □ Good throw! The men on shore have the ship tied up.

You hear the captain's order to line up around the deck. □ Find a place on the deck and stand at attention. The captain is very pleased with your work and thinks you are a good crew.

End music.

I think that you have worked so hard as sailors that you need to rest for a minute. Sit down on one of the chairs and we'll talk about being sailors. Which job did you like best?

Have a discussion. By your suggestions lead the children's thinking so that they talk about pirates who used to attack the ships and steal the cargoes, and of how the sailors had to learn to fight to defend their ships. Also discuss the point that in those days the sailors used swords because they didn't have any rifles or machine guns.

We forgot the fighting part of your sailor's training. Let's do it now. Stand up and hit the chair you were sitting on, hard with your fist. □ Which was hurt more? The chair or your fist? □ This time, see if you can bring your fist down hard to the chair but stop it just before you really hit the chair, so that you don't hurt your fist. □ Good. Now, using the chair as your partner get really mad at it and have a fist fight with it. See if you can win by not hurting your fist, not even once. □ You did! Now the chair is all covered with nails that need to be hammered in. Take a hammer and hit a different nail on each drumbeat. Use only one hand and use the other one to help you keep your balance.

Make loud, slow drumbeats, varied with some quick ones until most of the nails should have been driven in.

Good work. Each take a real partner and, to the drumbeat, have a fist fight with him in the same way as you did with the chair. Use your fist but don't let them get hurt. Just bring them up close to your partner. No one must touch any other child.

On the drum make some fairly quick steady beats. No child should be hit by another, but if anyone is hit, stop the exercise at once. Remind the children they have learned by using a chair as a partner how they can have a good fight with no need to actually hit the object or a person with their fists. Say that, in all our fights in a drama class—and we have some good ones in our stories—we know how to fight so that we never hurt ourselves, *nor any other child.* Let them try again if you have had to interrupt them. Continue with:

That was a good fight. Each of you fought so well that everybody won!

Now comes a harder part of your sailor's training. Pick up your sword, use it as though it were a part added on to your arm, and use your other arm for balance. Remember how long your sword is. Face your partner and begin sword fighting to the drumbeats.

This time mix some short, sharp beats with some slower steadier ones. When they have had a good fight, end the beats on the drum.

You are all dead. Fall down and relax. □

Have any of you ever heard of a man named Horatio Nelson? □ He was a very famous British sailor who commanded the navy in the days of sailing ships. There are books full of wonderful stories about his adventures on the high seas. But before he became an admiral, he had to learn, as a young boy, how to become a very good sailor and be a member of a ship's crew. I'll tell you the story of how Nelson, when he was a little boy, first learned to become a sailor.

Nelson was born in the northern part of England. He had six brothers and sisters. Their mother died, and they were brought up by a very strict father. Nelson loved his father, and even as a little boy he was not afraid of him as his brothers were. In fact, Nelson didn't seem to be afraid of anything.

His brothers were jealous of him and one day they teased him so much he got mad and started to fight with them. His father stopped the fight and punished Nelson because he had not been able to control his temper.

Not long after this, his Uncle Morris, the captain of a ship, visited them and promised to take one of the boys and train him to become a sailor. Nelson asked to be the one chosen. His uncle agreed and told him to come soon to his ship the "Iron Castle," which was in dock at Bristol.

When Nelson arrived at the ship, the other members of the crew found out that he was the captain's nephew, and that he wanted to become a sailor. They were very mean to him. They made Nelson do all their jobs: polishing the brass, scrubbing the decks, and peeling potatoes.

The captain told his first officer to teach Nelson the many difficult tasks which sailors have to learn, such as climbing the masts, crawling into the lookout, and hauling the heavy ropes to pull up the sails. The captain watched to see how well Nelson would do his work. And do you think Nelson lost his temper this time? □ No! Although he was often very tired and lonely and it was very hard work for a young boy, he did everything he was told and learned to do it well.

At last the captain told the first officer to send Nelson to his cabin. When Nelson reported to him, his uncle told him how pleased he was with his conduct and his work. He asked Nelson to be the midshipman, his special messenger on the boat. He became very fond of the boy and even taught him how to steer the big sailing ship. Nelson became the best midshipman the captain ever had, and it was then that he had his first adventure.

Out on the high seas one day, suddenly there was a loud shout from the lookout that a pirate ship was approaching. All the sailors got their swords and stood at attention on the deck waiting for the captain's orders. Nelson asked if he might be allowed to fight with the sailors to help protect the ship. His uncle knew that Nelson would be brave and gave him his first sword so that he might fight to save the "Iron Castle."

The pirate ship drew alongside, and the pirates shouted at the sailors to surrender the ship. Captain Morris gave the order, and all his sailors jumped over the sides onto the deck of the pirate ship. They fought hand to hand with the pirates, driving many into the sea and overpowering the rest of them. Nelson fought as hard and as bravely as anyone. It was a short fight, and very soon the pirate flag was hauled down from the masthead to be replaced with the British flag.

As a special reward for his bravery and daring during the fight, Nelson was allowed to steer the pirate ship while the "Iron Castle" towed it back to port and turned it over, along with the pirates who were left, to the authorities.

Now that you have all learned how to be good sailors of a ship's crew, as Nelson did, let's have two sailing ships and we'll do the story of his first adventure.

Divide the children into two groups. Assign one group to be the pirate ship's crew and name one boy as the captain. Assign the other group to be the crew of the "Iron Castle," and appoint one boy as Captain Morris. Another boy in this group will be Nelson. For these parts choose children whom you have noticed need encouragement to be leaders. Ask the captains to choose a first officer.

Now, everybody build the ships beside each other in the centre of the room, and then both the crews can get quickly to work.

If necessary, assist them to share out the equipment of chairs, tables, etc. for their projects. When they are nearly ready, hurry them along with a loud drumbeat and say:

One minute to finish your ships. □

As soon as the ships are finished, say:

Each sailor think of the work he will do on the ship, and start working at it. □ It is a nice day at sea and both the boats are sailing along. Captains, sail your ships; and first officers, see that all your crews are busy. □

Fade in the music, (A flowing rhythm, suggesting the sea. Suggested: "Play of the Waves," *La Mer*, Debussy.) to help them establish their work on the ships at sea.

Keep sailing your ships until you hear loud beats on the drum, and then Nelson will climb up into the lookout and sight the pirate ship. Then your adventure will start.

When they have their ships well established, give a loud beat on the drum and fade out the music. Your only job now is to see that nobody really gets killed in the skirmish that follows. If the fight goes on and on and on, suggest to the pirates that once they are captured they must stay captured, and that if they are killed they must stay dead. As a last resort, declare the fighting is OVER, and end the story quickly. When the story is finished, ask the children if they liked that adventure. If energy and time permits, they might like to do another dramatization of the story but do change around the ships' crews and appoint other captains and another Nelson. Girls enjoy doing this adventure as much as the boys do, and you can choose them for the leading roles this time. At the end of the lesson compliment them for fighting well for their ships.

FOURTEEN

Theme:

PANDORA'S BOX

Emphasis:

Developing children's concept of happiness

Materials: Drum.
Records.
 SUGGESTED: *A Walk in the Black Forest*, Jankowski.
 Peer Gynt Suite, Grieg.
 The Swan, Saint-Saëns.

Give a loud bang on the drum to gain the children's
attention and tell the children to "freeze."

Freeze! Each find a place on the floor with lots of
room around you, and lie down. □
Start the record. (A lively march. Suggested: *A
Walk in the Black Forest*, Jankowski.)

It is Saturday morning. You slowly wake up. □ It is
a beautiful day. Sit up and remember it is Saturday
— no school, a holiday! □ Quickly get out of bed and
dress in some fun clothes: old jeans, a sweater, a
pair of sneakers. □ Go into the bathroom; you don't
even have to wash very carefully today. □ A fast
brush of your hair and away you go downstairs for
breakfast. □ Look, it's your favorite breakfast. Eat
it up quickly, □ and run out of the house. □
You meet a friend and play a game of tag together. □
Try not to bump into other people. It's real fun to be
running and playing together. □ Each pair of
friends join up with another pair of friends. Play
leap frog over each other. □ Play follow the leader.
Who's leader? □ Walk along a railing. □ Jump up
and down some steps, □ think of anything else you
would like to do, or play together. □ You go to one
of your friends' houses, and there is a note on the
kitchen table. It says: "There are cold drinks in the
fridge and cookies in the cupboard." Get them out. □
Take them outside; sit down; eat and drink. □ Now
you are happy and tired. Lie down on the grass for
a rest.
Fade out the music. Discuss with the children their
experiences in the above exercise. What makes them
happy? How does it feel to be happy? What do they
feel like when several of them are happily playing
together?

Quickly find a partner and choose a place to work
together. Decide who is "A" and who is "B." □ "A"
is the city cousin, and "B" is the country cousin
who is coming to "A's" house for a visit. The two of
you have never met before. "A," open the door and
greet your cousin, who has just arrived, and take
him up to see your room, which you are going to
share. □
Allow the children to do this part, then continue:

Good. Now "A," show your cousin your favorite
possession. "A" must decide what it is; it could be a
toy, a book, a set you have collected or, whatever
you like best. "B" likes your favorite thing and,
while he is holding it, he drops it and it is broken.
What happens? Try that part together. □
Walk around while the children are doing this
exercise and observe their different reactions to the
situation. When they have finished, ask the children
to sit down where they are. Now ask one or two

61

pairs of children to share their work with the rest of the class. Choose for this pairs who have worked out contrasting endings to the same situation. Then, with all the children, compare the different endings, and discuss from their observation, the reactions of individual partners. Take care to ensure that the children note the changes of emotion accompanying these reactions.

Now, form groups of three and quickly decide which one is "A," "B," and "C" in each group.
Suggest the following three situations one at a time, and allow enough time for each one to be played out by the children.

(1) "A," "B," and "C" are good friends playing ball together. After they have played for a while, "A" misses the ball and runs out into the street to get it. He trips and he is knocked down by a passing car. Try doing this little story together and see what happens. Start to play ball together.□
When you see most of the groups nearing the end of this little scene, ask the children to sit on the floor as soon as they have finished doing their story. Discuss with the children what they did at the end and how they felt about the accident. In each of these short discussions held at the end of the three scenes, have the children describe their feelings when the story ended and contrast them with the feeling of "being happy" at the beginning of the scene. Allow only a few minutes for this discussion, then press on to the next situation.

(2) "A," "B," and "C" are friends and are all having fun playing a game of cards, such as "snap," or whatever one you like best. The friends each play a few cards, and then "B" is caught cheating at the game. Begin your game of cards together and see what happens. □
In the discussion with the children, inquire especially: "How did each one feel when "B" started to cheat?" "What happened at the end of the game of cards?"

(3) "A," "B," and "C" are good friends walking home from school together. When they reach "A's" house, "A" and "B" won't let "C" go into the house and see a secret project that they are making. Off you go. Walk together, and see what happens when you reach "A's" house.

In this discussion concentrate on how the various children worked out this situation and how they felt about it.

In the scenes you have done, what were some of the feelings that made you unhappy? □
Repeat the ideas the children suggest, such as being sad, being angry, feeling left out. Then continue:
Choose any one of these feelings. Now, to the music, you are the unhappy spirit of that feeling. Move any way you want to, spreading that feeling all around the room.
Start the record. (Wild, discordant music. Suggested: "Anitra's Dance," *Peer Gynt Suite*, Grieg.)

Away you go, and be as ugly as you like in your movements.
After a short while, stop the record and clap your hands.

Freeze! Now you are all the good spirits of happiness. Feel yourself becoming different from the unhappy spirit, as you fly spreading your happiness everywhere.
Start another record. (A graceful, flowing rhythm. Suggested: *The Swan*, Saint-Saëns.) Then, in a short time, fade out the music.

Well done, now fly over here. Sit down and relax while I tell you a story.
Did you know that a long time ago at the very beginning of people living on the earth, all the children were happy and had a very lovely life? They all stayed children and never grew up. There were no grown-ups to tell them what to do—no school, no dishes to wash, no jobs to do at all. Wouldn't that be wonderful? The children just played all the time. They each had a little hut to sleep in; they could pick all kinds of fruit off the trees when they were hungry; and they had plenty of clear cold water to drink when they were thirsty. One of the lucky boys who lived at this time was named Epimetheus, but his friends called him Eppy. Eppy had in his hut a most unusual box, which had been sent to him as a present. But it had come with a warning that it *must never be opened*. One day a beautiful young girl named Pandora came from another land to visit Eppy. Eppy and Pandora enjoyed being together. They shared the

hut; they played; they picked grapes and apples for their meals; and they never quarrelled. The curious box always stood in the corner, and often they wondered what it might contain. They used to play games guessing what the box could possibly have in it. Could you have guessed? □

Use the children's answers as you continue:

Yes, maybe it had toys, candy, jewels, or pretty clothes in it. But Pandora and Eppy always remember—what? □ Yes, that it should never be opened. One morning before they went out to pick oranges for their breakfast, Pandora asked Eppy to open the box just a little. She thought they could have just a little peek, and then they could close it up again. Eppy said, "No." Although Pandora coaxed and coaxed; what do you think Eppy still said? □ No! And he finally went out of the hut alone to get his oranges.

When Pandora saw that he had gone, what do you suppose she did? □ That's right. She was so curious, she thought just one look wouldn't hurt. She went to the box and began to play with the golden lock. It was an unusual lock, and as she worked to undo it, at times she thought she heard a sound coming from the box. Pandora was so busy trying to undo the lock that she didn't hear Eppy come back. He was sorry that he had gone out without Pandora; it was no fun being alone. He had brought back in his hands some oranges to give her for her breakfast. Eppy couldn't believe his eyes when he saw Pandora at the box, and before he had time to stop her, she unfastened the lock and opened the box! Suddenly the room became very dark and out of the box came all the unhappy spirits.

Mention some of the feelings of unhappiness that the children have experienced, such as sorrow, fear, and anger.

All these unhappy spirits moved around Eppy and Pandora and stung them and stung them, and they hurt the children very much. Eppy found the door of the hut and flung it open, and all the unhappy evil spirits went out into the once happy world. Poor Pandora was very sad that she had been disobedient, and she slammed shut the lid of the box quickly. How she wished she had never opened the horrid thing. She and Eppy were covered with stings and these stings were very painful.

As she sat crying in the dark, Pandora thought she heard a voice, which seemed to come from the box, saying, "Let me out, I'll help you!" Do you think she dared to open the box again? □ Well, at first she didn't want to, but this time Eppy thought he heard the voice too, and he suggested that perhaps they should open the box together. When they did, a beautiful white spirit came out who seemed to bring the sunshine and light back into the room again. She didn't hurt the children although she came near to them and even called the children by their names. Eppy and Pandora were very surprised because, as the spirit moved around them very gently, all their hurts from the stings one by one went away, and they felt happy again. The white spirit rested for a moment on the box again and the children asked her: "Who are you?" Who do you think the beautiful spirit was? □

Yes, she was the spirit of happiness. Then she told the children, "My name is Hope, and if you remember me when you are in trouble, I promise always to come and help you to be happy again." Pandora and Eppy were glad they had found a secret for always being happy again, no matter what happened to them. To this day, every time a child is hurt by an unhappy spirit such as sickness, sadness, or fear, if the child will remember that there always is Hope, a chance to be happy again, the spirit of happiness will come to him, too.

The children enjoy dramatizing this story very much, but it is helpful to break up the playing of the drama the first time. It is also desirable before they begin for every child to have the opportunity to experience being happy in a world of children. Otherwise, Eppy and Pandora are apt to take too long enjoying their happy existence while the "bad" spirits are shut up in the box. For this reason, if time permits, first have each child take a partner, and have each pair quickly choose a place for a hut. Tell them they are all good friends and happy children enjoying their world without adults. Start the children all asleep; they wake up in the morning and spend the whole day playing. When they are hungry, the children pick from the trees anything that they think they would like to eat. To end their day, suggest to the children that they are tired and they all go home to bed.

After the class have all been happy children, divide them into groups of 5 or 6 and let each group decide who is to be Eppy, Pandora, Hope, and the unhappy spirits. Have each spirit decide which feeling he will represent. Then the children make the hut, and Hope and the unhappy spirits make the box and conceal themselves inside it. The play commences at night time. In the morning, Pandora and Eppy wake up and they discuss the box. Eppy goes out to get some oranges and the action goes on according to each group's version of the story.

Observe their different versions. When most groups are near the finishing stage, give them a minute to finish up their work. If there is enough time to do the story again, let the children change the roles around in their groups and give the unhappy spirits a chance as Pandora, Eppy, and Hope.

At the end of the lesson thank the children for all their good work. Be sure to tell the children to remember the secret; that for each one of them, there is always a hope that can come to help them to be happy again when they are in trouble.

FIFTEEN

Theme:

THE SHOEMAKER

Emphasis:

Improving creative language ability

Materials: Drum.
Records.
SUGGESTED: *La Ronde*, Oscar Straus.
Carnival of the Animals, Saint-Saëns.

Call the class together with a loud beat on the drum.
At last it is cold enough for us to go skating! Go to your house and look for the skates that you had last year. □ Look in all the places you can think of where you might have put them away. □ When you find them, put on some warm clothes and carry your skates to the rink over here. □
Indicate the place.
Take off your shoes and try to wiggle your toes into your old skates. □ They don't fit? Never mind, I am bringing a big box of new skates to the rink.
Go over to the children, apparently carrying a huge box, and place it on the floor.
Throw your old skates in a pile over there. □
Indicate a place behind you.
Each child see if he can find a new pair of skates in the box that he would like to have and that will fit him. □
While the children are finding their new skates, question them as to what kind they want to choose and what size skates they need to fit their feet.
Sit down and try them on. □ Talk about the new

skates you have found to the person sitting next to you. □ Maybe you could help each other do up the laces tightly. Make sure that they can't come undone while you are skating. □
When all the skates are nearly on, start the record. (A familiar waltz. Suggested: *La Ronde*, Oscar Straus.)
The ice looks smooth. Now try out your new skates. Away you go, skate to the music. □ How well all the skates seem to work! Some of you can turn and do all sorts of fancy things. □ Careful, boys playing hockey! Try not to bump into the other skaters. □ I think you have skated enough for the first day. Go to the side of the rink and take off your skates. □
Fade out the record.
Someone must have gathered up all our shoes and taken them away. We'll have to walk home in our stocking feet. □
An appropriate drum beat will control the action.
Better run as fast as you can. □ When you get there, put on your best shoes, □ and walk in them, to form a circle in the centre of the room. □
Beat a walking rhythm on the drum. When they are all in the circle, give a loud drumbeat and say:
Sit down.
Join their circle yourself. After a general discussion on the shoes they chose to wear, ask some children, individually, to stand up and walk in their best shoes and describe them to us. Thank each of them,

and make a comment on their shoes based on what they have told you.

Now we are going to play a fun game. There is a magic box in the centre of our circle, and in it is every kind of shoe or boot that people would wear for walking, dancing, or playing any kind of sport. You can all take turns going to the box and taking out any pair that you can think of. Put them on and do whatever the shoes are made for. We will watch very carefully to see how you put them on and what you are doing in them, and we will try to think what the shoes look like. Then we will tell you what we think we see on your feet. Ready? Who can think of a pair of shoes that are in the box? □ John? Good. Go to the box, take out a pair of shoes, put them on, and show us what you would use them for, moving around inside the circle. □

The children take their turns. After each one has used the shoes for a minute or so, begin to ask questions, such as: "Who can tell what John is doing?" "What do you see on his feet?" "What do his shoes look like?" By your questions lead the children's thinking to explore their answers in detail. If some children, when their turns come, seem to lack ideas for various kinds of shoes, spur on their thinking with questions such as: "What kind of shoes do you wear when it rains?" "When it snows?" "What sports would you play in a playground?" "At the beach?" "In the wintertime?" When their attention begins to wane, continue:

Everybody stand up. □ To the drumbeat, we are going to walk in some more shoes. First of all, you have a new pair of shoes that are too tight and pinch your feet as you walk. □

Start a slow drumbeat and vary the rhythm according to the style of walk required.

Now walk in shoes with big long toes that flap as you walk. □ Now you have on shoes that have very high heels and you click, click, as you go along. □ And now you have on a pair of boots that come right up to your knees and are much too big for you. I think they are big enough to be your father's boots. □ It seems that we just can't get any shoes or boots to fit our feet. Just ahead of you is a shoemaker's bench with some leather and all the tools needed for making shoes. I think you had

better sit down and make yourselves a pair of shoes that will fit your own feet just right. Think how you could cut the leather and sew it to make your shoes. □

Use a record to aid their concentration. (Reflective music, with a definite rhythm. Suggested: "The Aquarium," *Carnival of the Animals*, Saint-Saëns.)

During this exercise, once it is well under way, walk around and talk quietly with individual children about the shoes they are creating for themselves. Be concerned with leading them to describe in detail the shoes they are making. When you sense that most of the shoes are finished, fade out the record. Then use drumbeats appropriate for the following actions:

Now that your shoes are finished, let's try them all on. □ They fit really well. Stand up in them. □ Look at them in the mirror. □ They are a fine pair of shoes! Now try walking in them. □ Maybe you can even skip in them. □ They still feel good? Let's jump in them. □ Now hop in them, all the way over here. □

Indicate the place.

Now, each take a partner, □ then each pair choose another pair of children to work with. □ We are going to try a really hard little game together. Decide on which partners are "A" and which are "B." □ In each group the two "A" partners have a shoe store. They can decide between them who is the owner of the store and who is the one who sells the shoes. The "B" partners are two people who go into the store to buy a pair of shoes for a child. They can decide who they are — such as, a child with a mother or father, or a child and a big brother or sister — and they must decide what kind of shoes they are going to ask for. "A" partners, quickly find a place to set up your store. □ When it is ready, the "B" partners will come to your store and buy the pair of shoes they want. Get to work, and let's see what happens. □

See that the children become involved as soon as possible, and observe the playing out of this exercise. When the groups have nearly finished, clap your hands and give them one minute to finish up. At the end of a minute, with a loud bang on the drum, say:

Freeze! Sit down where you are. Today we are going to have each group share with us the work they have been doing, and we'll begin with this group here. (Indicate one group.) Just do together what you were doing in your group, and the rest of us will sit quietly and listen.

At the end of their scene, thank them and if possible make a special comment about something you liked concerning their effort in working out their ideas. Proceed to the next group. Comment on each group's effort at the close of their playing; but do not single out any group as being "the best." They all have made their best efforts. When all the groups have finished, clap your hands and say: All come and sit over here. □ I know a story everybody can do together about a shoemaker. In a village there lived a shoemaker and his wife. One day he had only enough leather left to make one small pair of dancing shoes, so he cut the leather and went busily to work making the shoes. Now in this village there was a rich man who was called a lord. He lived with his lady and their four daughters in a big house. The girls were greedy children and, in spite of having so much, they always wanted everything they saw. The lord had a stable next to the house, and in it was a black shiny carriage and four white horses; and there were four footmen to look after the horses. Each day the footmen would hitch up the horses to the carriage. Then, with two footmen who sat at the front to drive and two who rode behind, they would bring the carriage around to the front door of the big house and take all the family for a ride in the village.

The footmen would get angry because they would go only a little way when they would have to stop the horses at a store where the daughters had seen something they wanted. Then the girls would pester their father and mother to buy it for them. On a certain day the dancing shoes were finished, and the shoemaker had just put them in the window when the lord's carriage came along. As soon as the girls saw the shoes, they begged their father to stop the carriage so that they could go in and try them on. The carriage was stopped. While the front footmen held the horses steady, the back footmen hopped down and ran around to open the carriage door.

The four girls ran into the shop to try on the shoes. The one pair fitted them all, and each child wanted that pair. What a noise they made quarrelling over who should have the shoes! At last the lord decided on a plan to keep them all quiet and to make them all happy. He gave the shoemaker some gold coins and told him to measure his daughters' feet, and then to make each of the girls a pair of shoes of any color they wanted by the next morning. At last all the daughters were content. The family got back into the carriage and drove home to have dinner and go to bed. The shoemaker bought some leather with some of the gold coins, and he and his wife started to work on the new shoes.

After the footmen, who were also magic little people, had bedded down the horses in the stable, they made a plan to teach the greedy daughters a lesson. Quietly they crept to the shoemaker's shop and looked through the window. They saw that as soon as the last pair of shoes had been finished, the shoemaker and his wife had fallen asleep at their bench. The footmen stole inside and, going to every pair of the new shoes, they cast a magic spell on each of the heels. The spell made sure that whoever should put on the shoes would be unable to take them off again and would be forced to dance all the time that the shoes were on her feet. I don't know how it was done, maybe you can think. □ Shall we let the footmen decide how to make this magic spell work when we do the story? □ Good. After they cast the spell, the footmen ran back to the stable and they were just in time, for it was already morning. That day everybody was up early. The footmen hitched up the carriage, and they took it around to the front door. The family got in, and off they all went straight to the shoemaker's shop to try on the new shoes. And what do you think happened? □ Yes, as soon as the daughters put on the shoes, they began to dance and dance all around the shop. The girls became very cross because their feet kept moving all the time, and they tried to take the shoes off. Do you think they could? □ No, the shoes were stuck fast to their feet.

The lord and lady started to laugh when they saw

their daughters hopping all over the place. The shoemaker and his wife began to laugh too, and they followed the family out into the street. When the footmen saw the daughters, they laughed at the joke, and even the horses joined in the laughter. When the family were back in the carriage, the girls' feet kept jumping up and down. The shoemaker and his wife followed the carriage, still laughing, and it seemed that everyone in the village was laughing at the daughters.

When the family arrived home and got out of the carriage, the daughters began to laugh. First they laughed at each other, and then they laughed at themselves for being silly girls and wanting everything they saw. That broke the magic spell, and the shoes stopped dancing. The girls remembered their adventure with the shoes and were never greedy again.

That is a story that will be lots of fun for us to do. Quickly get into groups of four.

Assign one group to be the horses and another to be the footmen. If there are any girls in the footmen group change them with any boys in the next group. The third group are the daughters.

Then in the fourth group we have Peter and Mary for the lord and lady, and John and Susan for the shoemaker and his wife. The shoemaker's store will be on the street here, and let's have the big house over there with the stable built close to it, here. (Indicate the places.) We'll have five minutes to build our houses. All of you help to make the place your group will need.

As the buildings near completion, clap your hands and say:

One minute to finish up. □

Then continue:

Each go to his place for the start of the story. □ We'll begin with everyone asleep. □ And now it is morning. First, we'll have the shoemaker and his wife get up and start to make a pair of shoes out of their last piece of leather. □ Then the footmen wake up to feed and brush the horses. □ And finally it is time for the rich family to wake up and get dressed for their ride. □ The footmen can bring the carriage around to the front door, if it is ready. □ Let's all try to listen to each other as we do our story.

If there is any confusion concerning the action at any point during the story, help the children out; otherwise, just enjoy their efforts. At the end of the drama discuss with the children their thoughts on the doing of it. If there has been too much over-lapping of dialogue, emphasize the idea that only one person should talk at a time. Each may take his turn to speak, but he must also listen to the others when they are speaking during the story. If the ''carriage'' proved awkward for the children to handle during the ride, let them try this part once again by itself, before you do the drama again. For the second time through the drama, don't change the children's roles; have them play the same ones so that they can achieve their experiences in greater depth. Begin the drama again in the same way as before. At the end of their playing, thank them for all the fun they put into their doing of the story about the dancing shoes.

SIXTEEN

Theme:

THE PARK

Emphasis:

Developing rhythmic movement

Materials: Drum.
Records.
SUGGESTED: *Mon Oncle*, Barcellini.
The Swan, Saint-Saëns.

Begin with a loud beat on the drum and say:

Freeze! Each child find a place to work in the centre of the room. ☐ Curl up as small as you can on the floor. You are all seeds of trees planted in the ground.

Begin a slow steady beat on the drum and continue:

To the drumbeat, you are going to begin to grow, and continue growing ☐ until the loud drumbeat. Then you will be a full-grown tree and will stand straight and tall.

Give a loud beat on the drum.

Good. A soft breeze blows through your branches.

Use an appropriate rhythm on the drum to suggest the following actions:

You sway from side to side, back and forth. It is such an easy-breezy feeling. ☐ Then the wind gets stronger and your branches are tumbled and tossed to and fro. ☐ Swish, swish, swish; it's harder to stand. It is a hurricane. Crash! You are broken off and you tumble to the ground. ☐

Good work. Curl up again very small and close your eyes. ☐ This time it is a sunny day, and you are the seeds of trees that have been planted in a park in the city. Listen to the drumbeat and try and grow a little each time the beat tells you to.

Begin with a medium steady beat and proceed:

Your roots creep, creep out, ☐ as you push through the ground. ☐ Now up, up, up! You grow taller and taller as your branches reach up to the sun, and now you are big shady trees standing in the park.

End the drumbeat.

Keep your eyes shut and stand comfortably. When I play the record, try to see in your mind's eye all the various things that are in the park and to notice what the people in the park are doing.

Start the record. (Any gay, lively tune. Suggested: the theme from *Mon Oncle*, Barcellini.)

Look down to the ground. Is there anything else you can see besides all the green grass? ☐ What games are the children playing on the grass? ☐ What are the paths made of, and are many people walking on them? ☐ What are they doing? ☐ What is making that gurgling sound over there? ☐ Do any of the children have anything in their hands? ☐ Why are some of them running? ☐ Did anything happen? ☐ What are all those funny shaped things behind you? ☐ Look around and see what else you can find that's interesting. ☐

Begin to fade out the record.

The sun is going down. Most of the people are starting to go home, and you are very tired as you stand there after such a busy day in the park. Go to sleep.

End the record and give a loud beat on the drum.

You are all released from your enchantment as trees; you are boys and girls again. Come over here and sit down.

Discuss with the children the sights they saw in the park. Try to encourage them to expand their imagination by asking questions that will require them to give greater attention to detail. You could use suggestions such as: "What trees did you see?" "What color and shape were the balloons?" "Tell us about the new bicycles." "What were in the flowerbeds?" "Who were some of the people you saw in the park?" "How were they dressed?" "What did they do?" "The fountain, what was it there for?" "Describe the fountain. Where did the water come from?" "What were the funny shaped things — swings? slides?" "What are they useful for in the park?" "What are the paths made of?" "What were some of the children doing on the paths?"

Everybody stand up. You are all the children whom you saw in the park. Get on your bicycles, and when the music starts, ride around the paths. □
Start the record again.

Watch where you are going. Steer carefully around the other people. □ Turn and go along another path; ride along as many different paths as you like. □ Good idea. Ring your bell if there is anyone in your way ahead of you.

Lower the volume of the record for each of the next suggestions that you offer the children. Then turn the volume up again for the action.

Park your bicycle. □ On the grass there are boys and girls playing kick ball. Join in their game. □ Kick your ball with your foot and run after it. □ Kick it again, and try not to lose your balance. Watch where it goes. □ Look, you have reached the playground area. There are swings, teeter-totters, slides, and a round-about. Play on any one of them that you want to. □ Wasn't that great fun? Now follow the flagstone path. Run along and jump from stone to stone. If you step on a crack, you'll break your mother's back! □ The path leads to the wading pool. Here it is. See if you can walk around the ledge. □ Good. No one lost his balance or fell into the water. Find a shady place on the grass and collapse.

End the record and give a loud beat on the drum.

Think for a minute about any lovely cool fountains that you have seen or can imagine. □ Mary, tell us about the beautiful one you can see when you think of a fountain.

Continue a discussion with the children concerning their fountains, and question them as to the different ways in which the fountains are constantly filled with water.

We'll divide into two groups and see if in each group, together, you can form yourselves into a beautiful fountain. Think how you might work together with flowing movements to suggest the water continually playing in the fountain. Then try making these movements to the music.

Divide the children into two groups, and give each group an area to work in. Start a record softly in the background to aid their concentration. (A slow, rhythmic tempo. Suggested: excerpts from *The Swan*, Saint-Saëns.) If necessary, assist the children to build on their ideas of a fountain. When they have made their fountain formation, turn up the record and give them an opportunity to practise moving together. When each group has their fountain working smoothly, stop the record. With a loud drumbeat, ask the children to sit on the floor where they are. Ask each group, in turn, to share with the class the ideas they have worked out and to make their fountain work to the music. Repeat the record for each group in turn, then comment on the group effort of building something together. Clap your hands and continue:

You are all taking a dog for a walk in the park. □ A cat appears, and your dog chases it up a tree. Make the dog sit down. □ Then try to coax the cat down the tree. □ When you get the cat down, pet it and send it on its way safely home. □ Go back to your dog, and then bring that naughty dog home here. □ Now put him in the back yard, and all come and sit down. □ There are cats and dogs in parks, but sometimes there are other animals too. Some parks have zoos. What kind of animals have you seen in a zoo?

Discuss with the children these animals, their habits, and their cages; talk about the animal keepers and what they have to do for the animals.

Let's make our own zoo!

Produce a loud beat on the drum to gain the children's attention.

Quickly get into groups of four. □ Decide in your group who is to be your partner. □ Then decide which partners are "A" and which are "B." □ One of the "A" partners is an animal of his own choice, and he is in a cage; the other "A" is the animal keeper. The "B" partners are two children playing in the park, and they can decide what game they are playing. Then the children visit the animal cage and talk with the animal keeper about the animal. They find out what the animal does, what it eats, and how the keeper takes care of it. Choose a place for your group and start to work. We will have just five minutes to do this.

Walk among the children at their work and observe their progress. At the end of the time, clap your hands and say:

One minute to finish. Then sit on the floor with your group. □ Good. Now we shall change around. The "B" partners are the animal and the keeper, and the "A" partners are the children. This time try to choose another kind of animal. The children can think of something else to play in the park at the start of the story. Again, we have five minutes for our work.□

After five minutes clap your hands for the children to finish, and ask them to sit down. For a few minutes, talk with them about the children's choice of animals, the animals' habits as talked about with the animal keepers, and the different forms of play chosen by the children at the start of the scene. Extend the use of their imaginations by asking the children to think about the variety of possibilities they used in the given situation.

All come over here, and maybe we can think of a story we can do together about some children in a park and some animals in a zoo. Who shall we say the group of children are? Do you think their teacher could have taken the children to the park for a special treat, or a special lesson? □ Any other ideas of why the children are in the park? □

Choose the idea that seems to be most popular among the children for the story and continue:

After lunch the children go to the zoo in the park.

When they are looking at the animals in the cages, they go over to the last cage and in it are the monkeys. The children laugh at them and play with the monkeys that are at the front of the cage. Suddenly, one of the monkeys, who is playing with the lock on the cage door, is able to open it! Maybe it wasn't properly closed when the keeper fed them the last time; however, the monkeys jump out of the cage, and they begin to play with the children. What are some of the things that the monkeys could do to tease the children? □ Everyone is having fun laughing and playing, but what about the poor keepers who have to try and catch the monkeys and put them back in their cage? What do they do? And what happens then? □

Accept one of the ideas suggested by the children to use for the ending of the story.

Now, for our zoo we will need several cages in a line with a big one at the end for the monkeys. And let's have two keepers to look after all the animals.

Divide the children into two groups, and indicate one group.

This group can make the zoo this time. You can start deciding who are the keepers and who are the monkeys, and you can build the cages in that part of the park.

Indicate the place, then to the other children say:

This group is the children (and teacher or leader if there is to be one), and they can decide how they want to work out their part at the beginning of the story. They can use this area of the room for their place in the park.

To all the children say:

We only have a little time, so see how fast you can get your places set up, and then we can begin our story.

When the children have set up their places in their respective parts of the park, begin the story. With a loud clap of your hands, say:

Everybody quiet, and now we are ready. The children in the story come over here to the entrance of the park and sit down. □ Let's say it is morning; the animals wake up and are fed by the keepers. □ The children go into the park. □

Let the drama proceed at its own speed. If it gets out of hand during, for example, the interplay between the monkeys and the children, stop the action for a moment and then suggest some way of finishing the story quickly. When the doing of the story is finished, ask everyone to sit down where he is, and discuss the story with them. Inquire of the children how they felt it had worked out; what they felt was the best part of the story and why; whether they could have worked together in any other way to make it better; and whether there is anything they would like to add to the story. If any of the following points need to be made, emphasize them to the children: they should not all talk at the same time; they have to listen to what others are saying in the story; when they are caught, they must help the story by staying caught; there must be no hitting or hurting another child in the scramble; they should watch what others are doing so they will know when it is their turn to play; and they will then each have a turn to do something and will also be able to think of other things they can do to help make the story a really good one.

Think of all the things we have been talking about and try tc see if we can do them in our story this time. Would you like to change the groups around when we do it again? □ Maybe you would like to choose some other kind of animals for the zoo, and maybe the children would like to choose something else to do in the park? Quickly decide in your groups, and we will begin in two minutes.

Allow the children time to do this. Ask for their decisions, and then outline to the class the version of the drama that is to be used this time. When the groups are in their habitats, begin the story in the same way as before, and continue with the children playing the drama to its end. At the close, if there has been any noticeable improvement in their teamwork, ask the children which one of the two dramas they enjoyed doing more. Have them appreciate that their greater enjoyment was due to the fact that each one listened, watched, and in his turn did interesting things in the story. Thank the children for their good work together.

SEVENTEEN

Theme:

THE SNOW QUEEN

Emphasis:

Awareness of the elements of winter

Materials: Drum.

        Tambourine (if possible).

Record.

    SUGGESTED: *The Snow is Dancing*, Debussy.

Begin with a loud beat on the drum and say:

Freeze! Do you remember when we learnt the word "freeze" at one of our classes? At that time we were all ice statues. □ What kind of weather do we have to have outside before we can make ice statues? □ Today we are going to think it is one of the first days of winter. It is cold, so you will have to dress warmly. When the music starts, all get ready to go out in the snow that is just beginning to fall.

Start a record. (A light, dreamy mood. Suggested: *The Snow is Dancing*, Debussy.)

See the light flakes of snow as they come down. Catch one on your hand and look at it closely. What shape is it? □ It melted. Catch another and see if it is the same shape. □ Hold it up to the sun and find out what color it is. □ It is snowing more heavily. Run in the snow and feel it as it hits your face. □ There is lots of snow. What could you make with it? □ All make a nice round snowball. Let's put the snowball on the ground and roll it along to make a bigger one. □ What could we use that for now? □ It could be the body of a snowman. Now we will need another snowball for the head. Let's make that, and then we will have the snowman all ready to put the

trimmings on. □ What kinds of things would we need to dress him up in? □

Use the children's ideas to suggest various activities, one by one, to do until the snowman is completely dressed. Fade out the record.

What a lot of interesting snowmen! Stand back and look at the one that you made. John, what did you use for his eyes? □ Describe the hat you found for your snowman, Mary. □

Continue to question the children about their individual creations of snowmen until you sense their interest decreasing. Then with a loud beat on the drum, proceed:

You are all now the snowmen you made! □ It begins to get dark, and the children go home. The stars come out and, at the hour of midnight, all the snowmen are very stiff from standing still so long. They begin to walk around. □

Use a slow heavy beat at the beginning of the exercise, then continue with appropriate rhythms for the further actions you suggest.

It is very hard . . . to move . . . your legs . . . and arms . . . they are . . . so big . . . and heavy. □ Now it becomes easier to move . . . your big . . . fat body. □ You can now walk faster and faster until at last you break into a little running trot. □ Now all the funny fat snowmen start to do a little dance. □ Suddenly it is morning; the sun is coming up, and all the snowmen scurry back to their places. □ They stand

still. □ They wait for the children to come out and play again. □ They wait and wait, and the sun gets hotter and hotter, and the snowmen begin to melt, little . . . by little, by . . . little, □ until all that is left of the big fat snowmen is a little puddle of water lying on the ground. □ (End the drumbeats.) If the north wind blew across that puddle, what could he make it into? □ What kind of a wind is the north wind? □

Ask several children for their answers until you have from them a detailed picture of the qualities of the north wind.

Everybody up. □ You are all the north wind, blowing fiercely around the countryside, freezing the puddles, and spreading snow as you go.

Use a heavy beat of moderate speed. A tambourine would be an asset here to suggest the falling and spreading of the snow.

Cover all the fields with snow; □ cover the roads, □ the fences, □ the rooftops, □ and the trees. □ What else can we cover with snow? □

Suggest, one at a time, the children's ideas for their ensuing actions, then continue with:

Now all the earth is covered with snow, and the north wind stops blowing and rests. □ What is the name of the wind that is the opposite one to the north wind? □ What does the south wind feel like when it blows? □

Discuss in detail with the children the qualities of the south wind — when it blows and from where.

Now you are all the gentle south wind blowing around the country and filling the air with soft breezes.

Use a light easy beat on the drum, or use a similar effect on the tambourine, and suggest:

How pleasant it is to float around, □ to blow through the tree tops, □ gently to blow the sails of the boats. □ What else could the south wind do? □

In order to stimulate their imaginations for the next part of the lesson, build on the ideas given by the children to suggest further activities for them as the south wind. Then continue:

Now it is evening, and the south wind gently dies down and rests. □ If there was a stray south wind that blew in the winter time, what would it do to the ice and snow? □ If there was a contest between the north wind and the south wind to see who could blow the hardest, which one do you think would win? □ Where do you think the north wind comes from? □ That's right, the far north. Does anybody know what the land in that part of the world is covered with for most of the year? □ That's right, snow! What is the name of the people who live there? □ What is one kind of house that the Eskimos live in? □ Do you know what the igloos are made of, and how they are built? □ How do the Eskimos get their food if there are no stores nearby for them to go to? □ What do you think they could do? □ What do the Eskimos use for travelling over the ice and snow? □ Do you think it is dangerous for them to travel over the ice and snow? □

Discuss Eskimos, igloos, dog-sleds, polar bears, blizzards, and ice floes with the children.

Let's divide into two groups. Each group is an Eskimo family who lives in the far north. Then you can make up your own story about a hunt for food.

Divide the children and allocate a place for each group. Then say:

Each child decide who you are in the family, then together you can build your igloo and quickly get to work on your story. We will have ten minutes to do this.

Help the children to iron out any difficulties that they may have in their work. At the end of the allotted time, clap your hands and give them a minute to finish up. After the minute clap your hands.

Sit down where you are. Shall we ask this group to share their story with us first?

At the end of the doing of this story, thank the children and comment on some idea that they have worked out well. Now ask the other group to share their work with the class, and, at the close, again comment on some work they have done well together.

Now, let's all do a story together about a Snow Queen who lives in the far north. We'll say she lives in a beautiful ice palace with the north wind and with all the little snowflakes who are the princes and princesses. Can you think of some of the things the snowflake children could all play or do together in the ice palace? □

Listen to the children's suggestions, then incorporate one or two of them in your story. Continue:

The snowflakes are having a wonderful time. Suddenly the Snow Queen looks at the calendar and sees it is December. She knows it is time for winter to begin again in the city to the south. The queen calls for the north wind and tells him to gather some snowflakes and get ready for the long journey south. Should we have all the prince and princess snowflakes go with the north wind? □

Choose one of the children's ideas as to how many or which snowflakes should go on the trip.

When all is ready, the north wind begins to blow and the chosen snowflakes follow him as he leads them on the long journey to the city. All the children in the city are asleep in their houses. In the night, the north wind and the snowflakes arrive at the city. He blows so hard and cold that the warm south winds shiver and run away. The north wind spreads all the snowflakes on the ground, then he rests near the houses.

In the morning the children wake up and look out of their windows. When they see the snowflakes, they are happy that winter has come again. They quickly dress in warm clothes and run out to play in the snow. The children make wonderful snowmen with the snowflakes. The north wind sees that the children are playing happily, and he flies back to the far north and makes his report to the Snow Queen that he has done his work and winter has started in the city.

But what about the south winds who are still hiding close by? Shall we have them be mischievous winds? □ All right, we'll have them see that the north wind has gone safely back to the palace in the far north. What could we have the south winds do? □

Use one of the children's suggestions in the story, then continue:

After that fun, the south winds come out of hiding, they blow all around the snowmen, and all the snowflakes begin to melt. The children are very sad. Now how can we have the story end? □

Decide on the ending from a popular idea supplied by the children, or suggest the following as an alternative.

The Snow Queen in her ice palace hears the unhappy signals from the children that the south wind is melting all the snowflakes. She calls the north wind and orders him back to the city to chase the south winds far away to their home in the south. When the south winds have gone, the north wind has to blow very, very cold air to turn the puddles into ice and to make the snowflakes again. When the children see the snowflakes have returned, they make snowmen with them and everyone is happy that winter has come to stay in the city.

Let's start to work on our story. Mary, you are the Snow Queen this time; John is the north wind; and this group is the snowflakes. We'll ask them to help build the ice palace over there. □ Peter and Susan are the south winds and the rest of you are the children in the city. Let's have it here, and you can make your houses in this area. □ See how quickly we can have all the places ready, and then we can start the story.

Help them to sort out any little problems that may arise, and when they are near completion of their dwellings, give them a minute to settle down quietly in their respective places. Begin the drama with the south winds blowing around the city. The children fall asleep and continue with the action of the drama in the ice palace. Let the children do the story in their own way. At the finish of the drama, discuss with the children their reactions to their playing out of the story, and ask them what they might like to add to it. If there was any difficulty during the playing out of the drama, help the children to sort out the problem and encourage them to try for a fuller group effort when they do it again. The children may wish to change their roles in a further re-creation of the story. Always talk with them about the work they have done in the drama, highlight any part that they have created well together, and thank them for their effort.

EIGHTEEN

Theme:

THE FIRST SETTLERS

Emphasis:

Developing awareness of history

Materials: Drum.
Record.
 SUGGESTED: *Lieutenant Kijé Suite*, Prokofiev.

Begin with a loud beat on the drum.
Quickly, each find a place to work in the room and sit on the floor. □ What is the name given to the people who lived in Canada before any white men came? □ You are all Indians. Take your bows and arrows and, to the drumbeat, walk through the forest and hunt for animals. □
Begin with a slow steady beat. Then using appropriate beats for the following actions, continue:
You walk quietly and listen to the sounds of the animals. □ Stop and listen. □ Was that a crackling sound of twigs and leaves? □ Something is moving over there; run lightly and chase the animal. □ There, you see it! Stop and take aim, then shoot an arrow. □ Did you kill it? Go and see if it is dead. □ What sort of animal is it? What will we do with it? □ Carry or drag it back to your tepee. □ Now what do we have to do before we can eat it? □ Good. Gather some twigs and wood for a fire. □ Light your fire. □ Now we need some bigger firewood to keep a good fire burning. Chop up some of the logs that you have beside the tepee. □ Skin your animal. □ Hang it over the fire and cook it. □ It is ready to eat. □ You must be hungry; have a feast. □ How else could the Indians get other food? □

Use the children's ideas for further activity. You might suggest that the Indians try: fishing, gathering berries, picking ears of corn, and later grinding the corn between two stones to make flour, and then mixing the flour with water to make small cakes to cook over the fire. When the children begin to lose interest, suggest:
What kind of animal skins did the Indians use to make their tents or tepees and clothing? □ Deerskins. Each go and hunt with your bow and arrow for a deer, and bring it back to the camp. □ What good hunting! Skin the animals and put the skins in the sun to dry. □ Does anybody know how they stretched them? □ That's right. Tie the skins on a frame made of strong branches. □ Now the skins are dry. We'll have the boys make tepees out of dried skins while the girls sew a jacket or dress and also moccasins for their feet.
Use a record suggestive of primitive music as a background for their concentration. (Suggested: *Lieutenant Kijé Suite*, Prokofiev.) Walk among the children and question them in turn about the work they are doing. When they have finished, suggest:
Now that we have so many wonderful tepees in our camp and all the clothes are made, everyone form a circle to join in an Indian dance. Johnny, would you like to beat the drum this time? □
Give several children a chance to be the drummer. Each child should announce a different kind of

dance he has chosen and beat the appropriate rhythm for rain, sunworship, harvest, planting, a war-dance, etc. When the children are physically tired, proceed:

All collapse on the floor; you are children again. □ How do you think the first people travelled to Canada from other lands? □ What did they call the people who came to settle in the new land? □ Did it take a long time for the settlers to cross the ocean? □ Yes. Many of them became sick, and they were very tired of the boat by the time they arrived here. Divide up into two groups, and each group can make a boat.

When the children have constructed the boats, clap your hands and say:

Sit in your boat, and you are the first settlers, crossing the ocean to come to the new land. □ Begin to think that you are really crossing the ocean, and try to work out a story among yourselves about what might happen to you and the other passengers while you are on the boat.

Have all the children begin their work at the same time. If they seem lost for purposeful action, use some of the following questions to suggest activities for them. Is it cold? Are you hungry? Maybe the food is running short? What happens if there is a storm at sea? The journey has been so long, do you suppose the captain has lost his way? If there are not enough sailors, would some of the passengers help on the ship? If one of the sailors fell overboard, do you think you could help to rescue him? Could the drinking water become stale and many people become sick from drinking it? Study the work of each group and select from the work of each an idea that you feel the children have become involved with and that they have worked out well together. At the end of ten minutes, clap your hands and give them a minute to finish their story. Then say:

All sit down on the floor where you are. This group were doing some very good work about . . . (mention the idea that you have selected).

We would like you to share it with the rest of us. Where would you like to start that part again? □ Good. Begin when you are ready.

At the end of their drama, thank them and compliment the group for their work.

I saw the other group working well together on a very interesting idea of . . . (mention the idea you have selected). We would like you to share that part of your work with us. Decide where you would like to begin and start when you are ready.

At the end, thank them and honestly appraise the good work you have seen.

Today, let's work out a story together about the settlers arriving in Canada and their first meeting with the Indians. □ Stay in your same groups. We will have this one as the settlers who will arrive on the boat. We'll use this boat that you've already made. Patrick will be your leader and can help you think which person you are who might be arriving among the first settlers and what new name you might like to have for the story. This group are the Indians, with John as the Indian chief, and they can make their camp over there. John will help you each decide who you are among the Indian tribe, and then you can choose an Indian name for yourself. Let's think that in each group there is at least one family, and then sort out what other people you might need to have among you for a story. Quickly get to work and we will begin as soon as you are ready.

After a few minutes, go to each group and listen to their ideas for the characters they have chosen. If the children have made happy decisions and are content with their roles, all is well. If not, encourage them to think of interesting ideas. A settler might be a nurse, a teacher, a soldier, or a builder. An Indian could be a hunter, a medicine man, a squaw, or a teacher of the young braves. Clap your hands to signal the finish of their preliminary work, and ask them all to sit down quietly.

Before we begin our story, we will ask each child to tell us who he is in his group and his new name if he has chosen one. First, the Indian tribe, and we have John — who is? □ And your name is? □ Then Mary, tell us who you are and what your name is? □ Repeat the new names to help make them more easily remembered and identifiable with the child. Continue until all the children of both groups have stated their chosen roles and names.

Thank you. Now we all know who each person is for our story. All go to your places, and let's begin with the settlers sitting on the boat, travelling quietly up the river. □ The Indians, who have their camp on a height of land further up the same river, are busy with their day's work— building a new shelter, making and mending canoes, finding firewood, cooking, and sewing clothes out of animal skins.

Allow the Indians' work to proceed until they have established the daily living pattern of their community. Then continue:

Now it's evening, and all the Indians sit around the camp fire and tell of their day's adventures.□

When this is well started, add the following narration to the story. Leave enough time in between each suggested action for the children to explore the situation in their own way.

One of the Indians hears an unusual splashing sound in the water; □ he goes to investigate the sound and sees the strange boat coming up the river. □ He reports this news back to the other Indians at the camp. □ They creep quietly to hide behind trees and wait to see what will happen. □ The settlers look out and see a landing place ahead of them at last. □ They are excited and talk about what kind of new land it is. □ They gather all their luggage and belongings, then prepare to go on shore. □ When they arrive, it is night time; they are tired and think of how and where they can all sleep. □ After the settlers are all asleep, one or two friendly Indians think they will go closer to them to look at these pale-faced people. □ This awakens some of the settlers, and they are frightened at the sight of the dark-skinned native people. □ The men get out their guns, but the Indians run quickly back to their camp. □

The women settlers don't want to have any killing or to be at war with the natives; they think of a plan to show the Indians they are friendly people. □ Some settlers are chosen to take the peace offering to the Indian camp. □ After this adventure, everyone sleeps peacefully for the rest of the night.

This situation could prove to be only the beginning of an adventure for the children; they often become so engrossed in it that not only do they want to repeat it often and in greater detail than before, but they enlarge the drama with many more exciting ideas. You may enjoy using some of them in a future lesson, or from the discussion you have with the children at the close of the drama, they may offer you some material that would fascinate them for further work. The following are a few suggestions to expand the drama:

1. When the settlers take the peace offering, the Indians, because they don't understand English, reject the gifts of jewellery with suspicion, and both groups retire to their respective camps to try and live their own lives.

2. One of the settlers' children is bitten by a snake while playing. The nurse is helpless to save the child; the mother goes to the Indian camp, and tries to plead with them in sign language to cure her sick child. After many awkward moments and events the child recovers.

3. The teacher begins classes for the settlers' children, and the Indian children shyly join them. Then the Indian children tell their people about the English language. The Indians want to learn more; it is a beginning of an understanding between the two groups.

4. The settlers need shelter, and so they study the Indians' tepees and try to make a similar one out of some of their belongings. It is unsuccessful. The settlers are forced to think how they should construct a dwelling such as a house which they have been used to living in.

5. The settlers' store of food they brought with them runs out, and they are very hungry. They become sick from trying to eat the berries and some of the animals they have killed. The Indian medicine man helps to cure them. The Indians share their knowledge about the food from the forest and streams and all the natural good food to eat that grows in the fields.

Note: It is best to try to steer the children away from a fight between the Indians and settlers, because there is more to be gained from the experience by leading their thinking toward establishing a social responsibility to community living. However, if the circumstances of their playing does evolve itself into a fight, let them get it out of their systems, and then offer, as an alternative, a peaceful solution to the situation. It is a very interesting unit. Enjoy it along with the children!

NINETEEN

Theme:

PERSEPHONE

Emphasis:

Awareness of nature in the spring

Materials: Drum.
Records.
SUGGESTED: *Peer Gynt Suite*, Greig.
La Mer, Debussy.

Begin with a loud beat on the drum.
Come over here and sit down. □ What are some of
the first signs outdoors that tell us spring is here? □
Listen to the children's ideas. If they do not introduce the subject of flowers coming to life again,
suggest it for their consideration. Continue:
It's spring again and all the flowers are in bloom.
When the music starts, go out into the gardens and
fields and pick a bouquet of your favorite flowers.
Start the record. (Delicate, romantic music. Suggested: "Dawn," *Peer Gynt Suite*, Grieg.)
Away you go! There are so many lovely flowers.
Look carefully among all the flowers to find the
ones that you like best. □ When you have gathered
your bouquet, come and sit down here with it. □
When most of the children have returned, fade out
the record. Discuss with the children the various
flowers they have picked and why they particularly
liked the kinds they chose. And ask them what we
do with flowers when we have picked them. You
might inquire of the children:
This is a beautiful bouquet, Mary. What flowers
have you in it? □ What do (roses) look like, John? □
Who brought back a different flower? □ Does it

have any leaves? What shape are they? □ Who has
some daffodils? □ What color are the petals, and
how are they arranged on the flower? □ What are
some colors of tulips you have seen? □ What shape
are their heads? □ Who picked another kind of
flower and what is it like? □ What would you like to
do with your bouquet, Mary? □ Who else could we
give our flowers to? □ Why do we like to give
flowers to others? □
When their interest wanes divide the children into
two groups.
Each child think of a flower that he can be. Now
see if your group can make a beautiful bouquet
together. Think of it as an arrangement of flowers in
a vase, and see how interesting you can make it. □
What gorgeous bouquets! Think very carefully how
you have placed your arms and body and head to
make your flower in the bouquet. □ Sorry, I forgot to
put any water in the vase. On the loud drumbeat,
all the flowers will droop, and then, to the steady
drumbeat, water will be poured in and we will see
if all the flowers can straighten up in the exact way
they are standing now. Ready.
Make a loud beat, then continue with a slow steady
rhythm until all the "flowers" have straightened up
again. End with a loud final beat.
Well done! Now look very carefully and notice
again where you are standing, and how you have
placed your hands and feet to help make the

arrangement. Now, on the loud drumbeat, each
flower break apart from the others in your group
arrangement and lie on the floor as an individual
flower.

Produce a loud drumbeat.

Good. Now let's see if, to the drumbeat, you can get
up and slowly move back into your same position
in the bouquet. Try to make only one move with
your body to each beat, and end up standing in
exactly the same way as before and help to make the
attractive arrangement again.

*For this action, use a steady, rather slow beat until
all the children are back in their "arrangements."*

A very good try. Relax where you are. □ We have
been talking about the flowers that you can grow in
gardens, but what do you call the little yellow
flowers that grow wild and bloom all over the lawns
in the spring? □ Yes, dandelions, and there are
always so many of them. Run and pick as many of
them as you can.

*Give some fast beats on the drum; then, ending
with a loud beat, say:*

Freeze! What could you make with all those
dandelions? □ Do you suppose you could sit down
and make a long chain to go around your neck or
put on your head? Try it. □ Some of you work very
fast; I am sure your chains are long enough to put
on now. □ There, you are all real little flower-
people! □

How many know of a small furry animal called the
groundhog? □ He sleeps all winter in a deep hole in
the ground, and early in February, they say, he
wakes up and crawls out of the hole. Does anyone
know what he comes out of his hole to see? □ He
comes out to see if he can see his shadow. If he can,
he knows that it will not be spring for six more
weeks. Isn't that funny to come out to look for a
shadow? □ Have you ever seen your own shadow? □
When can you see it? □ Stand up and see if you
can find your shadow on the floor. □

*You can use the electric lights to help the children
make shadows with their bodies.*

You found it. See how many different ways you can
make your shadow move as you stand there. □

For this exercise use drumbeats of various rhythms.

Could you make your shadow dance? □ Try and

catch it. □ Isn't it fun, making it move exactly the
way you do? Good work. Sit down and rest where
you are. □

In the spring we hear the songs of birds that have
returned after the long winter. But close your eyes
and listen to this record, and see if you know
another sound that tells us spring has come again.

*Start the record. (A rippling, water sound. Sug-
gested: "Play of the Waves," La Mer, Debussy.)*

Listen carefully and think what, out in the country,
would be making the same running sound as that? □

Fade out the record.

Who can say what sound of spring that music
reminds us of? □

*Accept any of the children's answers pertaining to
water. Use their idea "of water" as a springboard to
begin a discussion of the flow of water. Emphasize
that, as the ice and snow melt, the water forms little
streams. These join up with other streams which
become rivers, and eventually the rivers flow into
the lakes and oceans.*

We will play a game. You are little springs of water
asleep under the snow. See if each one of you can
wake up and join the flowing stream to become a
big river; and finally together you are the big waves
of the ocean, the children of the sea running up on
the shore and back again. Everybody find a place
and make a very large circle in the centre of the
room. □ Stretch out your arms and have plenty of
space between you and the next person. □ Turn
around and sit down facing the wall. □ All the
springs are fast asleep, and we will start our game
with John, who will be the first to wake up. He will
walk around the circle and when you think he
passes you, you will wake up and join in the
movement of the river around the room. All ready. □
Shut your eyes and listen carefully.

*Start the record again to provide background for the
action.*

John, start any time you want. □

*When the child selected has completed the circle, if
there are any children still asleep, awaken them so
that they, too, can join in the action. Fade out the
record, and say:*

Freeze! A very good try. Most of you did listen well.
Back to your places, and we will do it again. □ At the

finish this time, John, have the river run across the room here, (Indicate the place.) and all of you, to the drumbeats, become the waves of the ocean. Try and keep together in a line, and think of the waves as being sea children who run up on the shore and back again. Shut your eyes and we will begin. ☐

Start the record. When the children are standing in their positions across the room to form the ocean, begin a slow heavy drumbeat.

Try to keep together. In . . out. In . . . out, ☐ and freeze.

Stop the record.

Relax. Well done. With the sun for our light we can see all the wonderful things on the earth, but have you ever thought what it is like under the earth? ☐ Do you think it is light or dark? ☐ What kind of materials or treasures could we find there? ☐

Discuss with the children minerals such as gold, silver, iron, copper, coal, and talk about their uses.

In the olden days men used to dig for these minerals by hand. Artists made many wonderful objects out of them. Some of their beautiful work we still see in museums today. At that time people didn't have cars to get around in, but they used to have chariots. Does anyone know what a chariot looks like? ☐ It was like a big open metal can set on wheels, and it used to be pulled by horses. They could drive very fast in them, and sometimes they had chariot races. Do you know, I think if we got in groups of three, we could make a chariot. Let's try it. Quickly get in threes. ☐ Now, two stand in front and link your inside arms; you are the horses. ☐ The driver stands, facing the same way, behind these two. ☐ He takes the free hand of each of the two in front to use as the reins. ☐ Right, now try to move slowly together and see if the driver using the reins can have the horses turn the way he wants them to go. Just walk and try not to let go of your hands or bump into another chariot. ☐ Good work. All the chariots move up to that end of the room and we can have a chariot race. ☐ Line up. ☐ And away you race to this end of the room. ☐ Please change drivers now, and then we can race back. ☐ All ready. Off you go. ☐ Now, the last child to have a turn, change to be the driver. ☐ On your mark, ready, set, go. ☐ And all collapse on the floor. ☐

I thought we could do today a story about why we have a winter and a spring each year. Many years ago there was said to be only one season. It was summer all the time. Wouldn't that be wonderful all through the year? Mother Nature used to look after all the flowers blooming and the crops growing. She had to take many trips all over the land to see that everything grew well. Mother Nature lived with her daughter Persephone in a little house near the sea. One day Mother Nature was leaving on one of her trips, and she told Persephone to play in the garden but not to go into the fields. Persephone asked if she could go and play with the sea children. Her mother said "yes," but the girl was not to be away for long because she herself would be back from her trip before dark. Persephone went down to the sea to play with the sea children.

After a while they grew tired of their games and Persephone thought it would be fun to gather some flowers and make chains. The sea children couldn't leave the water and go into the fields with her to gather flowers or they would die, so she went alone. Do you think she should have gone? ☐ No, her mother had told her not to.

As she was tugging at some flowers, a remarkable thing happened. Around the flowers the earth suddenly fell away and made a big deep hole, and out of the hole came a golden chariot with two fiery horses and a driver who was dressed in gold. He told Persephone he was Pluto, king of the underworld, and asked if she would like to go for a ride in his golden chariot. What do you think she did? ☐ She said "No"! The king, although he was a very kind man, was also a very lonely man, living by himself, and he wanted to have some company. So, he grabbed poor Persephone into his chariot and off they went.

Persephone screamed, but they were going so fast that no one helped her. They passed a boy playing a flute for the flowers to dance to, and an old woman in a cave. On and on they flew until they came to the entrance to the underworld palace of Pluto. It was very dark, lit only by the sparkle from all the jewels. The door of the palace was guarded by two fierce dogs. Pluto was the only person who could pet the dogs, and he was the only one they would let go through the door. Persephone held Pluto's hand, and she was very frightened. Together they went into the palace. Pluto called a servant to bring Persephone anything she wanted to eat. The poor child was so unhappy she couldn't eat, and she knew that, as long as she was in the underworld, she mustn't eat any of its food.

Mother Nature returned to her house and, though she called and called for Persephone, there was no answer. Do you all think you could help her call Persephone? Try it. □ Where could she go first to try and find her? □ She could ask the sea children. Mother Nature hurried to the sea and asked the children if they had seen her daughter. What do you suppose they told her? □ Yes, that Persephone had gone to the field to pick flowers.

Mother Nature ran to the field, where she met the boy playing his flute for the flowers that danced. He stopped playing and told her that he had heard some screams and looked up to see a golden chariot with a girl in it racing in the direction of the caves. Mother Nature ran to the caves. She asked the old woman if she had seen the chariot. What could the old woman tell her? □ That's right, she had. Then the old woman told her it was Pluto's chariot and he was off to his palace in the underworld, but the palace was guarded by fierce dogs who would let no one enter.

Mother Nature was so sad she sat down with the old woman and made a promise that nothing should grow again on earth until Persephone came back to her. Soon all the flowers stopped growing and lay wilted on the ground. The boy who played the flute went to the cave to see Mother Nature. She told him of her promise that nothing should grow until Persephone returned from the underworld. The boy offered to bring Persephone back to earth. For the journey, he put on his sandals, which had magic wings on them so that he could fly right over the fierce dogs and into Pluto's palace. Before his arrival Pluto had just given Persephone a pomegranate as a treat from above the ground, hoping that she would eat it. Without thinking, she ate six of the seeds. When the boy came in and told him how sad Mother Nature was and pleaded with him to let Persephone go, the King made a plan. He

would let Persephone go back to her mother, but, because she had eaten the six pomegranate seeds, she would have to spend six months of every year with him in his underworld palace. Everyone agreed to this plan, and so Persephone flew back with the boy. When she walked on the earth, all the flowers started to grow again.

Mother Nature saw the flowers starting to grow and knew that Persephone must have returned. She ran home to greet her daughter. Persephone told her of King Pluto's plan. And that is why to this day we have a winter season when nothing grows on the earth, and it is said that Persephone is in the underground palace of Pluto. When she returns to her mother on earth it is spring and all the flowers bloom and everything grows once more.

That's a wonderful story to do. Quickly get into groups of four, and we'll begin working at it. □

In the following sections appoint individual children for each of the various roles as you name them, and indicate the location of each group's working area.

We'll have this group for Pluto, the servant, and the two horses for the chariot; they can build their underground palace here. □ Then in this group we can have Mother Nature and Persephone, who can make their house here. □ Mary, would you be our woman in the cave here? □ And John, you are the boy who plays the flute in the field over there. □ Now, let's have these two children for the mad dogs at the entrance to the palace, and the other two children can join John and they are the flowers who dance in the field. □ Then this group are the sea children, and we will have the beach here next to the field. Get your places set up and we can begin. □

Because this story is rather complicated, it may be necessary to give the children a fair amount of assistance with the doing of it for the first time. Be helpful, and give the children enough narration to enable them to keep the action going at a good pace. If the dialogue and interest in any part of the story show that the children have become deeply involved with that situation, allow them to play it out at their own speed. When all their habitats are constructed, clap your hands.

Everybody ready to begin? Everything is very still, □

and we will start our story at the house of Mother Nature, who tells Persephone that she has to go on a short trip.

At the completion of the drama, say:

You did that very well. Would you like to do it again and see how much of the story you can remember by yourselves this time? □

If there are any children who seem unhappy with their roles, change them around. However, if a child recreates a familiar role, it will give him a greater sense of accomplishment. At the end of the drama this time, congratulate the children for their good work together, and tell them how well they remembered so much of that wonderful story.

NOTE: Provided your and the children's interest is sufficient, this drama is one that lends itself to further development in another lesson. At the close of your class today, ask the children to think about some other things that they could do to add to their parts for the story next week. Next time, after a short discussion, you can begin with the playing of the drama and continue it for the entire class. Do not aim for a theatrical production, but help the children to work out their new ideas so that they can incorporate them into the drama. They will experience a great deal of joy from their own creative efforts.

TWENTY

Theme:

THE LIVING GODDESS

Emphasis:

Developing control through ritual movement

Materials: Record player, drum, and eight additional "musical" instruments. These can be a tambourine, cymbals, two pieces of wood, rice in a closed tin, a tin can or box with a rubber band stretched across the open end, a string with several screw tops from jars on it to jangle, pot lids, etc.

Records.
SUGGESTED: "Polovtsian Dances," *Prince Igor*, Borodin. *Scheherazade*, Rimsky-Korsakov.

Foreword to this unit: The people of Nepal are of Indian descent and, although they are of a more primitive nature, the customs and culture of the country are Indian-oriented. The two important factors that the children should understand during this lesson are: that the way of life is based on manual labor and is centred around the Hindu religion. This is a religion of peace and absolute trust in the god Shiva. At the temples, the people express their love for him with continual individual prayers, gifts of flowers, and festivals of music and dance. The temple thus becomes the community centre for its people. In Nepal, the people of the country pronounce the name with a short "e" and the stress is on the last syllable: Ne-pahl.

Before the class, build a "temple" by placing chairs so that they form a large hollow square and make only one entrance. Devise an "altar," solid enough for a child to stand upon, in the centre of this square.

Close by, outside the "temple," construct a "fountain" of a rectangular shape.
Make a loud beat on the drum to gain the children's attention.

To the drumbeat, run around the chairs. □
Begin with a very fast beat, then gradually make it slower and slower. End the drumbeat and say:
Now come over here and board the waiting airplane. Sit down and fasten your seat belts. □
Today we are going for a very long trip to a far country. The name of it is Nepal. Can you say that? Ne-pahl. □ Good. Ready for take-off, and away we go! Lie back, shut your eyes, and relax as we go across the Atlantic ocean, over the countries of Europe, and high above the mountains of northern India. At last we can see the icy peaks of the Himalayan Mountains. Down below us is a lovely valley. It is in the little country of Nepal. We have landed safely. Unfasten your seat belts and walk off the plane. □ To the music, let's start exploring the country and meeting the people.
Start a record. (Any music suggestive of the East. Suggested: "Polovtsian Dances" from *Prince Igor*, or *Scheherazade*, Rimsky-Korsakov.)
It is very warm, and all the people we meet seem to be very tanned from the hot sun. How sparkling their dark eyes seem in contrast to the white of the saris that the women wear. The men look cool in their tight white pants and loose shirts or jackets.

See some of the people leaving their little houses of mud brick with thatched roofs and walking toward the temple. A temple is their place of worship. There it is, the square building in the centre of the town! Look at it closely. What do you suppose all the wood carvings represent? □ There are several roofs, one above the other, pagoda-style. Notice all the little bells around them. Can you hear the tinkling sound they make when they are blown by the wind? □ Look at the big bronze figures of the animals that guard the entrance! □ How strange, the people are all removing their shoes before they enter the temple. We had better do the same. □ Now, go in and walk quietly around inside the temple. □ Isn't it unusual that there are no chairs or benches to sit upon? In the centre is the golden colored altar. Such a lot of flowers the people have placed on the beautiful little statues of the gods and goddesses that stand around the walls! □ Shall we go out again into the street? □ Don't forget your shoes at the door. □

There are so many people in the streets. Some of them travel in rickshaws or on bicycles, but most of them walk. The women carry water jugs on their shoulders and fill them at the fountain near the temple. Do go over there to it. □ There are some children bathing, rubbing their feet and hands with stones to get them clean. See the woman doing her washing. How hard she beats it on the stones at the edge of the fountain. □

Now let's wander past the open market beside the temple. Men and boys with yokes across their shoulders are carrying hanging baskets of their wares; other people are squatting on the ground beside the goods they have for sale. Such a lot of different things to buy: brass pots, water jugs, silks, jewellery, fruits, and vegetables.

Would some of you like to be our market people? □ Good. This group squat on the ground beside your wares. □ You are the native people of Nepal. Start to call out in the native language the names of the goods you are selling. The rest are tourists who will buy something from you. □ When you have selected your purchase, ask the native to deliver it to you and come back to the hotel over here. □

Indicate the place. When most of the children are finished this exercise, fade out the record. Ask them to gather around for a discussion of this eastern country. Encourage the children to explore the East, its people, their costumes, and their customs. Suggest they might use any previous knowledge of the East they may have, or some ideas they have imagined from the foregoing narration. As their interest wanes continue:

Each take a partner and find a place to work. □ Quickly decide who is "A" and who is "B". □ "A" is a native child of Nepal—a Nepalese, and "B" is a Canadian child on a visit. First, the Nepalese will teach his partner the greeting used in his country. He puts the palms of his hands together with the fingers pointing upward toward his chin, and with a slight bow of the head, says: "Nahmahstay." "A" try it, palms together, then a bow of the head and say: "Nah-mah-stay." □ Good. Now teach it to your Canadian friend. □ How quickly he learns! "A," take your Canadian friend for a walk in the village, and when you meet another couple, greet them. □

At the end of this action, with a loud beat on the drum, say:

Freeze! Good work. The Nepalese use their hands a great deal in all their actions. All sit down on the floor facing your partner, with your legs crossed, and we'll try some hand movements together. □ "A," put your hands up in front of your face with the palms turned out as if you were placing them on a window pane. □ "B," you are on the other side of the glass, put your palms matching your partner's, but just not touching, for there is the glass between them. □ Keeping your hands in that position, to the music, "A," see how many different patterns you can trace on the glass with the palms of your hands, and "B," see how well you can follow and reflect your partner's hand movements on the glass. □

Start a record, a slow rhythmic excerpt from the previous selection. After a few minutes duration, fade out the record.

A very good try. Now stand up, face each other, and place your hands in the same position with the palms almost touching. □ Remain standing still, and this time, to the music, "B" is going to trace the patterns with his hands, anywhere upon the glass that stands between you, and "A" is going to reflect his partner's movements. ▫

Start the record, using the same excerpt, then shortly fade out.

How well you are all working together. Give your hands a good shake, ▫ then put them back almost together again. ▫ This time "A" will lead again, and "B" will follow. We are going to move to the music, first facing each other, then turning back-to-back, and then turning to face each other again. Always make sure that your hands reflect those of your partner, and that they almost touch when you are facing each other. ▫

Start the record again. After a short time reduce the record volume.

Now, still thinking there is the glass between you, with the palms of the hands almost touching each other, "B" move your arms and body to the music. You may go anywhere you like in the room. And "A," see if you can follow your partner's movements exactly as if you were his reflection. ▫ Turn the music up again, and continue until the children's concentration begins to wane. Fade out the record. Collapse on the floor.

That was some very interesting work you were doing together. I have in this box some simple musical instruments. Would each "B" partner quickly pick one out when I come around to you? ▫ You are all going to help me make an orchestra. Just sit where you are and everyone listen. First of all, let's start with a simple rhythm of some one, two, three beats. All the "A's" get ready to clap with me when I beat on the drum for the first beat, then the "B's" will make the second and third beat on their instruments. Ready.

During the following exercise always use the drum as required to lead the children.

And One-two-three, One-two-three, One-two-three. ▫

Continue as above but without vocally giving them the beat, then make a loud beat and say:

And freeze! This time "B's" sit cross-legged on the floor, ready to supply the second and third beat. "A's," stand up in front of your partners. All the "A's" on the first beat will bend their knees and pick a flower with their right hand; then stand up again. Pick one from the floor, on one side of your partner, then move your right arm over his head and pick one from the other side of him. All ready, begin: One side, two, three. The other side, two, three. Back again . . . And again . . . One . . . One . . . And now try your left hand this time. Ready. One, two, three. The other side, One . . . One . . .

Continue this action a few more times without vocalizing the beats, then make a loud beat and say:

Freeze! The left hand is harder to use, isn't it? ▫ Change places with your partner. ▫ "A" will have the instrument and be our orchestra for the second and third beat, and "B" will move to the beats in a circle around his partner. On the count of "one," "B" will bend his knees and pick up a flower, first with the right hand on his right side, then stand again, and walk on beats two and three. Then bend again, and with your left hand pick a flower from your left side. Continue in this way, alternating your hands each time. Let's try it slowly. Ready? Bend your knees and pick with your right hand from your right side. And walk, two . . . and three. Then bend and pick with your left hand on your left side, and walk, two . . . and . . . three. Again, right, two . . . and . . . three. And left, two . . . three, and freeze!

Good. Now, we'll try it to a little faster rhythm. Everybody listen to the music, and try to keep in time with it. Ready, and . . . Right, two . . . three. Left, two . . . three. Right . . . Left . . . And one . . . And one . . . ▫

Continue to build the speed until the children have a nice, free, flowing style. Then make a loud beat and say:

Freeze! Very good!

Now "A and B" change places again. ▫ This time "B" has the instrument and sits on the floor with his legs stretched out in front of him. "A" stands at his partner's feet. ▫ We are going to use four beats this time, one on the drum and the two, three, and four beats on the other instruments. On the first beat, "A" is to stamp his right foot on one side of his partner's leg. Then, "A," lift your foot over your partner's legs while you hop on your left foot, for the count of two, three, and four. Now, stamp your right foot again on the other side of your partner's legs on the one beat, and, still hopping on your left leg bring your right foot back over to the first side. Try it once or twice together, slowly doing your own counting. You must not touch your partner's legs. □ Any problems?

If there are any problems, let the others practise while you help sort out the difficulties. For this exercise, use a rather quick beat to help the children keep their balance.

Everybody ready? Let's begin. One . . . two . . . three . . . four. Stamp, two . . . three . . . four; stamp, two . . . three . . . four. One, two, three, four. And one . . . And one . . . And freeze!

Quickly change places. □ "A" is the orchestra, and we'll make it hard for "B." He'll use the left foot this time to stamp and lift across his partner's legs, while he hops to the beats on the right foot. Try it several times. □ Good, and away we go. Stamp, two . . . three . . . four; other side, two . . . three . . . four. One, two, three, four. One . . . One . . .

End beating the drum with a loud beat.

And freeze! You were all very good.

Will you please put the instruments back in the box, and everyone come and sit here. □

Indicate the place.

Today, I thought we could do together the story of one of the beautiful festivals that the people of Nepal take part in each year at the temple. It is the festival of the Living Goddess.

At this festival the priests choose one of the girls of the village to become a "living goddess." They also choose two other maidens to be her attendants, and together they live in a beautiful palace until the festival comes again the following year. We'll begin our story on the morning of the festival.

All the girls wake up and are very happy that the day has arrived. Quickly they carry their water jugs to the fountain for fresh water and, while they are there, they wash themselves for the great day. The girls greet their friends, and there is much excitement in the air.

When they return to their homes, each girl puts on her most lovely sari and decorates her costume with many garlands of flowers. Each girl walks alone to the temple. When she enters, she says a little prayer to the gods at the altar and offers them a gift of flowers. Maybe each girl prays that she may be the one chosen at this festival. After this, she finds a place to sit on the floor in a large circle around the altar, and she waits.

In the meantime, in a large dwelling where they all live together, the priests are also getting ready for the festival. They awaken and put on their long brown robes. They choose their musical instruments, and together they form a line for the procession. As soon as the maidens are all seated in the temple, the priests begin their procession through the streets, playing their instruments as they walk. When the priests enter the temple, they chant a prayer together at the altar. Then, they move to the far end of the room where they sit on the floor. Everyone is ready for the festival to begin.

Let's do the story that far, then add to it the festival inside the temple. The temple is all ready in the centre of the room. The streets of little houses will be around it, and the priests' dwelling can be here.

Indicate the place.

Would you like some music for a background during the drama? □ I'll do that part. The boys will be the priests and can go and make their dwelling; and each of the girls may choose her house on the street along here.

Indicate the place.

Quickly get set, and as soon as you are ready we can begin.

This preparation will require only a short time. Clap your hands and say:

Good. Finish up. Now lie down quietly in your place, and be asleep. Then we will begin our drama.

Use the same recording that you used at the beginning of the lesson. It should be played at a low volume to allow for any dialogue from the children.

It is the morning of the festival! Everybody awakens and the day begins.

Allow the children to do the drama in their own way, but always be helpful if they are stuck. At the conclusion of the drama, discuss with the children their ideas of how they felt it worked out and what they could suggest to improve their work together when they repeat it. Ask them if they would like to do this part again now, or suggest that they might like to complete the story and try the second part of it, then do it all from the beginning. Follow their wishes in making your decisions at this time. The completion of the story is as follows:

The festival to celebrate the choosing of the Living Goddess begins. The priests begin to play a simple rhythm on the instruments. All the maidens rise and do a dance together around the altar. Then each maiden, in turn, performs a short dance to the gods before the priests. The maidens end the dance together by all gracefully sitting in the circle again. Now the priests, except the orchestra leader who plays the drum, get up and they perform some movements at the altar to a ''one, two, three, four'' beat to learn of the decision from the gods. After this, to the same beat, the high priest leads the other priests among the maidens.

The two maidens who will wait on the Living Goddess are chosen first. They rise and go along with the priests. Finally, the head priest chooses the maiden who is to be the Living Goddess. The priests lead the maiden to the altar. Her two attendants adorn her with garlands of flowers, then the priests lift her gently up on to the altar, and they bow down around her. The rest of the maidens take the flowers from their own costumes and place them on the altar around the Living Goddess. She is then lifted down from the altar and the festival ends when the Living Goddess is taken, along with her two maidens, to a beautiful palace where they will live for the following year. I think that's a wonderful festival to know about from Nepal.

Inquire of the children:

Would each group like a few minutes to work out their dance movements together for their part in the story, or shall we begin and see what happens? □

Follow the children's decision. If the groups want some time first, allocate a place for each group to work and give them a musical instrument to use. Otherwise, continue with the action from a suitable starting point in the drama. It is often a more rewarding experience for the children if the story is done in this broken fashion and later all put together, rather than being completed in one continuous action. It gives the children a sense of security to first create their movements, then incorporate them along with the suspense which will build toward a climax for the drama. In order to maintain the excitement and suspense of the drama, have the priest's decision of the Living Goddess kept a secret by the high priest. This decision should be changed each time the doing of the play is repeated. In further work on this story, include any good suggestions offered by the children from your discussions at the finish of their playing of the drama. It will give you a great joy to share their creative efforts.

TWENTY-ONE

Theme:

HALLOWEEN

Emphasis:

Developing awareness of folklore

Materials: Drum.
Records.
   SUGGESTED: *Peer Gynt Suite*, Grieg.
   Firebird Suite, Stravinsky.

Give a loud beat on the drum to gain the children's attention.

Everybody come and sit over here. □ What are some of the costumes you will wear on Halloween? □ Each put your costume on. □ Now, by magic, you are the person or thing of the costume you are wearing. Leave your house, and begin to move through the streets. □

Start a record. (Heavy, mysterious music. Suggested: "Hall of the Mountain King," *Peer Gynt Suite*, Grieg.)

Meet your friends. □ Call on several houses. □ Now come to my house over here. □

When they all arrive, fade out the record.

What do children say when they go to a house on Halloween? □ (Shell out, trick or treat.) "Shell out" is a fairly new phrase we use, but the idea of "trick or treat" has been with us for many hundreds of years. The idea was first thought of by the Celtic people. They lived in Ireland, Scotland, Wales, England, and parts of northern Europe a long time ago. Halloween was the last day of their year, the same as our New Year's Eve, but it came at the end of autumn, before the change to winter. It was celebrated as the night set apart for spirits.

Now, there were good spirits and bad spirits. The good spirits were the ghosts of the people who had died. On this night, the Celtic people believed, they would come out of their graves in the cemeteries, go to their old houses, and visit with the relatives who lived there now. The families would know that the ghosts would be coming on that night, and they would prepare a feast as a treat for them. I don't know whether any member of a family could actually see the ghost of one of their relatives when it came to the house, but some thought they did. Let's try a few scenes and see what might happen. We'll think that the good spirits are in their graves in the cemetery over there. (Indicate the place.) And when the clock strikes six, the ghosts come out of their graves and pay a visit to their old house. The family will be there and will make a feast for them. They have their visit together and, at the sound of the clock striking twelve, the ghosts return to the cemetery and rest in their graves for another year. Each group can decide which relative of their family the ghost might be, whether anyone sees him or not, and what could happen during the visit. Quickly get into groups of four, think who you are in your story, find a place for your house, and start working together. We'll take ten minutes to do this. □

Walk amongst them during this time and help the children to sort out any difficulties. One of each group is the ghost and the other three are the relatives. Encourage each group to devise its own sound effect for the chiming of the clock. When most are finished the doing of their story, give them a minute to finish up, and then ask all the children to sit quietly on the floor.

Let's share one or two of our "treat" stories of the good spirits. This group was doing a most interesting idea they had worked out together. We'll ask them to share their work with the rest of us. ▢ Begin any time you are ready.

When you ask children to share their work with the class, use only good examples of group effort. This will spur all the children to think up and carry out better creative work during their exercises together. At the finish of a group's story, thank them and commend them specifically on their work. After the last group you have chosen is finished, continue:

Let's now think of the other part of the phrase we use on Halloween — the "trick." The Celtic people — do you remember who they were? ▢ Good. You did. These people knew that, as well as good spirits, there were bad spirits abroad in this world. They believed that on this night the bad spirits took the form of witches and wizards. These creatures would swoop through the air from place to place on broom-sticks or ride over the countryside on their black cats, which were turned into fast black horses for that night's mischief. The witches and wizards were always dressed in black from head to toe, so no one could ever see them when they used their magic powers to play tricks on the people in the dark of the night. What mischief they did! Besides teasing the people to frighten them, the witches and wizards have been known to steal all the wood that people had stored for the winter; or sometimes they would turn all the cattle loose from the barns into the fields; and it was thought that, if there were any children out, they would be lost forever, for the witches and wizards would turn them into animals or other creatures. Certainly the witches and wizards were a bad lot, and all the people were scared of them and usually stayed indoors on that night.

I think all the people are safe in their houses. Let's all be wicked witches and wizards. Shall we start to get dressed? ▢ What would we need to put on to cover us all in black from head to toe? ▢

Repeat the children's ideas, to itemize the costume for everyone to put on.

There, you've made yourselves invisible; I can't see anyone. When the music starts, all get on your broom-sticks and fly away into the dark of the night.

Start the record. (A fast, exciting rhythm building to a climax. Suggested: *Firebird Suite*, Stravinsky.) After a few minutes, lower the volume of the record, and say:

What place shall we visit first? And what tricks shall we play on the people? ▢ Wouldn't that be fun! Let's all try that.

From the children's ideas choose one and get them to carry it out. Turn the volume up for the action. When the children have finished the doing of one idea, lower the volume and ask them to suggest another, and then stimulate them into the doing of that. You may see one child carrying out an interesting idea of his own, and you could suggest it for everyone to try. If they need stimulation for their imaginations, suggest one or more of the following actions. Tip-toe up to a door and knock loudly on it, then hide; when the door is answered laugh loudly and fly away again. Steal a piece of clothing from the washing of the clothesline, and make it look as if it were dancing around by itself. Slide under the door of the candy store, choose a big box of your favorite candies, and sit down on the floor and eat them all up. Now our tummies are so fat, how are we going to get back out again? Take the baskets of leaves that the people have gathered up and scatter them back over all the lawns again. Collect all the pumpkins you can out of the fields and put them on the fence posts. Pump buckets of water and pour them down the chimneys so that the people can't light their fires.

Finish this section with the witches and wizards casting a magic spell over their cats and turning them into fast black horses to ride far into the wood, back to their secret meeting place. When all the children have arrived at the indicated place, ask them to sit on the floor. Then fade out the record.

They say that all the black-magic tricks are done by

the witches and wizards when they gather at their secret place deep in the woods. Usually they have a partner to help them perform their magic. What kind of magic trick can you think they might do? □ Each of you take a partner and choose an idea between you for a magic trick. See what you can work out together, and then we will have a magic circle and you can perform your trick for all of us.

Give them a few minutes to work out their ideas. If one pair need extra people for their idea, you might suggest teams joining up, or you might ask another pair, who may be floundering for an idea, to help them out. When they are nearly finished working together, clap your hands and ask all the witches and wizards to sit in a magic circle. It is great fun if you enter into the spirit (no pun intended) of the scene and, with a long pointer, go into the centre of the circle, and say:

I am the Master of the Black Rod, and, in the presence of all the witches and wizards, we will begin our secret meeting tonight with the magic trick of Wizards John and Peter.

Each group should perform their trick in the centre of the circle. You might suggest that the rest of the children hold hands around the circle if they wish to keep their magic in. When each pair finishes performing their trick, lead the applause and comment on their effort. Proceed with equal enthusiasm to the next couple until all the children have had their turn.

Now the dawn is coming up, the wonderful night is over. When the sun rose, the Celtic people used to gather together and light a big bonfire. This fire destroyed all the bad spirits. The father of each family would take a torch from the bonfire and with it light a fire in his home. That is how he could protect his family during the long winter. The fire would keep them warm, and it would also keep away all the bad spirits caused by quarrels, sickness, or hunger in the home.

I'm sure they have lit the bonfire; my magic rod is just a stick again! The magic circle is broken! You are no longer witches and wizards, but wonderful children! Thank you for all your good work.

Theme:

THE PALACE TWIST

Emphasis:

Developing awareness of others

Materials: Drum.
Records.
SUGGESTED: *Pictures at an Exhibition*, Moussorgsky.
The Sleeping Beauty, Tchaikovsky.

Before the lesson place in a large oval arrangement enough chairs to allow one for each child in the class. Make a loud beat on the drum. Then use appropriate rhythms for the following actions to gain the children's attention.

To the drumbeats walk around the chairs with as big and as long a step as you can. □ Walk with your legs as far apart as you can. □ Walk with as short and as quick a step as you can. □ Walk over here on your tiptoes as quietly as you can. □

If you were in a beautiful palace, what do you suppose the throne room would look like? □

Have the children describe what kind of floors, rugs, chairs, walls, windows, draperies, ceiling, lights, and statues or paintings they imagine there might be in a throne room.

You are all maids and manservants in this gorgeous palace. Take your feather duster and to the music dust all the beautiful statues and paintings and tables that you see in the throne room over there.

Start the record. (A lively rhythm. Suggested: "Ballet of the Unhatched Chicks," *Pictures at an Exhibition*, Moussorgsky.)

After a short time, lower the volume and proceed

with the following exercise. Each time, lower the volume to make a new suggestion, and then raise it again for the action.

I think everything is dusted now; put your dusters away. What would we need to clean the rugs? □ Good. Each take your vacuum and clean the rugs. □ How well you did that! Put your vacuums away. What other part of the floor still needs to be cleaned? □ Of course, the marble floor. Everyone take a pail and cloth to scrub it. □ How lovely the floors look when they are sparkling clean again! Don't miss any spots. The royal housekeeper is bound to notice and make us do our work over again. □ All done? □ Good. Put the pails back. What else is there to clean in the throne room? □

In the order they give them to you, use the children's ideas to suggest actions such as polishing windows, cleaning mirrors, and cleaning brass. End this exercise with each child taking a soft whisk to brush gently the velvet-covered chairs with golden legs. Then say:

How hard you have all worked! Everything seems to be very neat and clean. Sit on one of the velvet chairs and look around the room. See how well you have cleaned everything.

Fade out the record.

You are so tired, you shut your eyes and fall asleep. □ You dream that you are a prince or princess.

Fade in the record. (Music suggestive of serene

splendor. Suggested: "The Waltz," *The Sleeping Beauty*, Tchaikovsky.)

You look magnificent in your royal robes. Think what color of gown or suit your are wearing. ▫ You put your hand up to your head to see if your jewelled crown is there. ▫ It is. You are a real prince or princess. Open your eyes, get up and walk around the throne room. ▫ Think of the crown on your head and try to walk so tall and so smoothly that it does not move one little bit. ▫ When you meet another prince or princess, give a slight bow, or curtsey, to greet each other. Don't let your crowns slip. ▫ Now, go to one of the elegant chairs, turn round, and sit without losing your crown. ▫ Good. How straight and tall you are sitting in your chairs, with every crown still in place.

Fade down the record.

What do you suppose the princes and princesses would do all day, if they had to stay indoors in the palace? ▫ I think so, maybe they would . . .

Repeat some of the ideas the children give you. Or suggest to them such activities as: study, read books, play chess, listen to music, embroider or sew, play a musical instrument, practise dancing or fencing.

It is raining outdoors: you have to stay in the throne room. Think of something that will amuse you for a while and do it. ▫

Turn the record up for the action each time, then lower it while you are speaking.

You have done that for a while: it no longer amuses you. Try something else. ▫ You lose interest again; what else can you think to do? Try it. ▫ Nothing seems much fun; you become bored, and finally you just sit on the chair. ▫ Close the room out by shutting your eyes. ▫ The little golden clock chimes the hour.

Produce this sound by striking a cymbal or tin can several times, and end with a loud sharp beat.

You wake up out of your dream, and you are yourselves again.

Fade out the record.

When we think of princes, princesses, or kings and queens, we immediately see them dressed in their royal robes, their special costumes of royalty. Mary, can you describe for us the costume you imagined you wore as a princess? ▫

With questions that show your interest in their costumes stimulate their imagination by having the children describe the details of the costumes that they think they wore as princes and princesses. Lead their thinking so that they also describe a costume that a king or queen might wear.

Now think hard. Can you describe what kind of costume a maid in the palace might wear? ▫ What other names are given to the menservants who work in a palace? ▫ What kind of costumes would they (footmen, butlers, equerries, or page-boys) wear? ▫ A great many people wear a special costume or uniform for their particular job. Can you think of some of them? ▫

Encourage the children to see for themselves that, in fact, most things we do in the form of work or play can be identified by the costume worn.

Each take a partner and decide which is to be "A" and "B." ▫ "B" is the costumer in his store and "A" comes to the store to order a new costume to wear at his work. "A" can think he works at any job he chooses, but he must remember to order everything he will need to wear: shoes, gloves, and hats as well as the dress or suit. Quickly get to work, and we will have five minutes to do this.

Observe them at their work. When they are finished, clap your hands and ask the children to sit quietly on the floor with their partner. Select several groups who have demonstrated good examples of the exercise to share their work with the rest of the class. When they have finished, point out the good thinking that was shown by the itemizing and descriptions of the costumes. Comment on the way in which the children listened and responded to each other in their work.

Now, let's have "A" as the costumer in his store and "B" as a prince or princess who comes to order a new outfit for a ball that he or she is attending at the palace that very night. Think of all the things you would like to have for your completely new costume. Begin right away, and we will have five minutes.

This time, since you have outlined the good work shown by one or two groups in the previous scene, there should be a general improvement of all the groups. If time permits, allow each group to share their efforts and emphasize the good points about their work.

I know a fun story that we can all do together about some servants and some royal children in a palace. Each day the royal housekeeper would wake the servants early, and as soon as they were dressed, before they had any breakfast, their orders were to clean the throne room. The royal housekeeper was very strict. She seemed to have eyes everywhere and could see any spot of dust or dirt on anything that was not cleaned well. When the servants had finished their work, the royal housekeeper would line them all up while she inspected the throne room. If she agreed that it was clean, their next job was to awaken the royal children, help them dress, and serve them breakfast; finally, when the children left for the throne room, the servants had to make their beds and clean their rooms. They were so busy working all the time, never did the servants have a chance to rest.

On the other hand, the princes and princesses would enter the throne room and greet their father, the king, who sat on the throne. He was always very busy with the court affairs but, because he loved to have his children around him, he would tell the children to sit on the golden chairs and amuse themselves until later, when he would have some time for them. That time never seemed to come. The children would have to sit and wait such a long time that they became very bored trying to amuse themselves. They longed to be able to do some work. The poor servants had too much to do, and the princes and princesses had too little to do.

One day the king had a surprise for his children. He was going to give a masquerade ball for all the people in the palace! And, yes, that very moment, all the children could go to the royal costumer and choose any costume they wished. Then they were to keep their costumes a secret from him until they appeared that night in the throne room for the ball. How excited the princes and princesses were as they hurried to the royal costumer to choose their outfits. Because they had so little work to do and envied the servants who were always busy, they knew what clothing they wanted to wear. What costumes do you suppose they chose? □ You guessed.

All the royal children chose servant costumes. Meanwhile, the king called the servants in to the throne room. He invited them to the ball and told them that they could have the rest of the afternoon off to go to the royal costumer and choose any costume they wished. Because all the servants longed to be able to do nothing all day, they knew what clothes they wanted. What kind of costumes do you think they chose? □ Yes. Each one chose the costume of a prince and princess.

When all the guests were dressed in their costumes, they entered the throne room and the ball began. There was music and dancing and a wonderful feast that everyone enjoyed. At the hour of midnight, the king declared the ball was over.

The servants went with the royal children to help them to undress for bed, and a most peculiar thing happened. As soon as they undid the buttons, the buttons did themselves up again. As soon as they untied one shoe to take it off, it tied itself up again. And try as the servants would to remove the children's clothes, as fast as they undid anything to take it off, it did itself up again. The royal housekeeper came to see what all the noise was about. She was most upset. She told the royal children to go to bed in their clothes and sent the servants to their rooms to undress themselves. When they started to remove their crowns what do you think happened to them? □ The same thing; the crowns slipped back on their heads again. □ So what did the servants have to do? □ They were so tired they lay down on their beds and slept in their clothes. In the morning the situation became worse. When the royal housekeeper awakened the servants so that they could start cleaning the throne room, each of them not only was still wearing the costume of a prince or princess, but believed that he or she had become a prince or princess! And the servants would do no work at all! They would only sit on the golden chairs in the throne room. The royal children awoke with a start, still in their servant costumes. Who do you think they believed that they were? □ They believed that they were the servants. Quickly they ran into the throne room and started to work to clean it up. The royal housekeeper didn't know what to do.

When the king entered the throne room, he was very annoyed to see his children still in their costumes and doing all the work. He ordered each one of them to sit on a golden chair at once! The king sat on the throne and thought about the problem. He discussed it with the royal housekeeper. They wondered who could have played this trick on them all. The trouble began with the costumes, that was certain. There could be only one person to blame. Who do you think it was?

The king sent for the royal costumer. He questioned him about the costumes. Yes, the costumer admitted, that he was the one who had played the trick. He knew that the servants were unhappy because they had too much work to do, and that the royal children were unhappy because they had too little to do. The costumer promised to remove the clothes and make everything right again, if the king would promise to agree to a good plan for the palace people. The king thought about this, and when everyone in the throne room begged him to accept the offer, he finally agreed. The costumer told of his plan; everybody agreed it was a good one and order was restored to the palace.

You will be begged to reveal the plan, the missing link in the story, but it has been left out on purpose. Use the children's enthusiasm to encourage them to enjoy the mystery.

The costumer's plan? It's a surprise, only the costumer knows. Shall we have John as our costumer? Because there are so many costumes to be made, would Peter like to help him?

Choose for the costumer a child who has leadership qualities. Allocate the other roles and indicate each location as you mention them in the following section:

Then we need a very strict royal housekeeper. How about Mary for that job? Then there is the king. All right, Jimmy, you are the king. And do you think we might need a queen to help with all the royal children? Jane is the queen. This group of children are the servants, and the remaining children are the princes and princesses. We'll use these chairs that are already in an oval shape for the throne room. The king and queen can make their throne at this end, and the entrance to the room will be down there. Let's say the servants' rooms are at this end of the palace: the royal children have their rooms over there, and the king and queen have this place for their bedroom. The royal costumer can make his store in this area, next to the palace. Quickly help build your places, and then we can begin our story.

After you have helped the children to sort out the available materials and they are busily engaged, discuss with the two costumers any ideas they might have for the plan. Ask them to think what plan they might make if they knew one group had too much work to do and the other had too little work to do. If the costumers agree that the work and play in the palace should somehow be shared, have them devise a plan to remedy the situation. Then, to enable the children to remove the costumes, the costumers should think of some magic, as a talisman which everyone could touch, or that they give everyone a tablespoonful of cod-liver oil from a large silver bowl, or any other fanciful scheme that would fit the bill and is feasible to carry out in the drama. When the story is repeated — and the children will love building on this situation — change the roles around and challenge the new costumers to think of different ideas for the plan and the magic. Meanwhile, as soon as the places are nearly set up, clap your hands and tell the children: It is night time. Everyone is asleep in his room. ▫ In the morning, first of all the royal housekeeper awakens. ▫ Then she goes to the servants' rooms to awaken them, and the day at the palace begins.

Allow the children to proceed with the action in their own way. If they seem unsure, or if one particular action goes on too long, or you see signs that they need some stimulation to regain their concentration, suggest the next action for them. At the close of the drama, share their enjoyment of the surprise ending and commend the costumers for their idea. Discuss with all the class their reactions to the playing of the story, and the part they enjoyed the most and why. Ask if there are any parts they would like to improve, and how this could be done. Are there any changes or additions they would like to make? Do they wish to change parts and have fun doing it again? Each time they repeat the drama, encourage the children to expand it by using their own suggestions. Always remember to thank them for their wonderful ideas and their good work before they leave your class.

EPILOGUE

These units are now complete, but they are meant only as an introduction to Child Drama. Now that you have experienced the scope and potential of this approach to education, it is hoped that you will be able to provide your children with many more opportunities to explore the world and themselves through the practice of *draosophics*,* or learning by doing.

*AUTHOR'S NOTE: Educators and others who use drama as a learning device have asked for a new word to describe and cover the entire scope of "learning by doing." We offer the term *draosophics*, from the Greek words *drao*, "I do," and *sophikos*, "pertaining to wisdom." Thus *draosophics* means the science of gaining wisdom through the experience of "doing" in all its many phases from childhood through adulthood.

171304

SUGGESTED RECORDS

Individual recordings and catalogue numbers have been listed for the convenience of teachers. In most cases, however, several other recordings are available, any of which would be equally satisfactory.

LESSON	TYPE OF MUSIC	SELECTIONS AND ALBUM TITLES
THE FOREST	smooth-flowing, pastoral	*In a Monastery Garden*, Ketelbey (London CM-9041). OR *The Trout Quintet*, Schubert (London 6090).
THE FAIR	lively medley of gay tunes	"Victor Herbert Favorites," from *Concert in the Park*, Boston Pops Orchestra (RCA Victor LSC-2677).
THE CIRCUS	quick march simple rhythm with clear instrumentation	"Tiger Rag," from *The Percussive Twenties* (London P54006). "Mack the Knife," from *Percussive Oompah* (London P54009).
THE CAVES	flowing rhythm, suggesting the sea	"Play of the Waves," from *La Mer*, Debussy.*
THE FIRE	fast, exciting rhythm building to climaxes	*Firebird Suite*, Stravinsky.* (*Firebird Suite*, Columbia ML-4700, includes *Pictures at an Exhibition*, Moussorgsky.)
A TIGER HUNT	rhythmic, suggestive of jungle	*Carnival of the Animals*, Saint-Saëns (RCA Victor LM-2075. This album includes *Peer Gynt Suite Nos. 1 and 2*, Grieg.)
THE PRINCESSES' PEARLS	light, rhythmic, suggesting bird sounds	"The Cuckoo" and "The Aviary," from *Carnival of the Animals*, Saint-Saëns (RCA Victor LM-2075).
LANDING ON THE MOON	light, floating rhythm modern, electronic	*I'm Forever Blowing Bubbles*. *2001: A Space Odyssey* (original soundtrack: MGM S1E-13-ST). OR *Selections from 2001: A Space Odyssey*, Bernstein (Columbia MS-7176).
SWITZERLAND	lively march	*A Walk in the Black Forest*, Jankowski (United Artists UAL 3556).
THE OLD HOUSE	sprightly, mysterious reflective, mysterious	"Ballet of the Unhatched Chicks," from *Pictures at an Exhibition*, Moussorgsky.* (*Pictures at an Exhibition*, Columbia ML-4700, includes *Firebird Suite*, Stravinsky.) *Jeux — poème dansé*, Debussy (Columbia ML-5671).
THE TOYMAKER	ballet	*The Nutcracker*, Tchaikovsky (Westminster XWN 18223).
THE PRINCESS AND THE FROG	graceful, flowing courtly, elegant stylized, bright	"The Swan," from *Carnival of the Animals*, Saint-Saëns.* OR *Greensleeves*, Vaughan Williams.* *Rhapsody on a Theme of Paganini*, Rachmaninoff.*

LESSON	TYPE OF MUSIC	SELECTIONS AND ALBUM TITLES
NELSON, THE BOY SAILOR	majestic, building to climaxes	*Walküre: Ride of the Valkyries*, Wagner (Columbia MS-7246).
	light, suggesting the sea	"Play of the Waves," from *La Mer*, Debussy.*
PANDORA'S BOX	quick march	*A Walk in the Black Forest*, Jankowski (United Artists UAL 3556).
	wild, discordant	"Anitra's Dance," from *Peer Gynt Suite No. 1*, Grieg (RCA Victor LM-2075, includes *Carnival of the Animals*).
	graceful, flowing	"The Swan," from *Carnival of the Animals*, Saint-Saëns.*
THE SHOEMAKER	familiar waltz	*La Ronde*, Oscar Straus (Capitol SP-8603).
	reflective, with definite rhythm	"The Aquarium," from *Carnival of the Animals*, Saint-Saëns (RCA Victor LM-2075).
THE PARK	gay, lively	*Mon Oncle*, Barcellini (Capitol SP-8603).
	graceful, flowing	"The Swan," from *Carnival of the Animals*, Saint-Saëns.*
THE SNOW QUEEN	light, dreamy	"The Snow is Dancing," from *The Children's Corner*, Debussy.*
THE FIRST SETTLERS	rhythmic, suggestive of primitive music	*Lieutenant Kijé Suite*, Prokofiev (Odyssey 32160084).
PERSEPHONE	romantic, delicate	"Dawn," from *Peer Gynt Suite No. 1*, Grieg.*
	rippling, suggesting the sea	"Play of the Waves," from *La Mer*, Debussy.*
THE LIVING GODDESS	music suggestive of the East	"Polovtsian Dances," from *Prince Igor*, Borodin.* *Scheherazade*, Rimsky-Korsakov (RCA Victor VICS-1444). OR *Scheherazade* (Angel SFO-36034. This album includes "Polovtsian Dances," from *Prince Igor*, Borodin.)
HALLOWEEN	heavy, mysterious	"In the Hall of the Mountain King," from *Peer Gynt Suite No. 1*, Grieg.*
	fast, exciting rhythm building to climaxes	*Firebird Suite*, Stravinsky.*
THE PALACE TWIST	sprightly	"Ballet of the Unhatched Chicks," from *Pictures at an Exhibition*, Moussorgsky.*
	serene splendor	"Waltz," from *Sleeping Beauty*, Tchaikovsky.*

*An asterisk indicates that the selection is included in one or more of the following collections:

*FOR THE YOUNG IN HEART/MUSIC THAT PAINTS A PICTURE
RCA Victor LSC-2713 stereo
LM-2713 mono

"Ballet of the Unhatched Chicks," Moussorgsky
"The Swan," from *Carnival of the Animals*, Saint-Saëns
"The Snow is Dancing," from *The Children's Corner*, Debussy
"Play of the Waves," from *La Mer*, Debussy

*FOR THE YOUNG IN HEART/MUSIC TO TELL A STORY BY
RCA Victor LSC-2766 stereo
          LM-2766 mono

        "Waltz," from *Sleeping Beauty*, Tchaikovsky
        "In the Hall of the Mountain King," from *Peer Gynt Suite No. 1*, Grieg
        "Infernal Dance of King Kastchei," from *Firebird Suite*, Stravinsky

---

*REVERIE
Columbia MS-6575 stereo
          ML-5975 mono

        Greensleeves, Vaughan Williams
        Rhapsody on a Theme of Paganini, Rachmaninoff
        "Dawn," from *Peer Gynt Suite No. 1*, Grieg
        "Polovtsian Dances," from *Prince Igor*, Borodin
        "Clair de Lune," from *Suite Bergamasque*, Debussy

---

*THE CHILDREN'S CORNER and SUITE BERGAMASQUE (Debussy)
Angel 35067

        "The Snow is Dancing"
        "Clair de Lune"
also:
        "The Little Shepherd"
        "Golliwog's Cake-Walk"
        "Serenade for the Doll"
        "Jimbo's Lullaby"

RECOMMENDED READING

Barnfield, Gabriel,
Creative Drama In Schools.
London: Macmillan, 1968.

A book written for teachers of Child Drama, which analyses their role as leaders and gives an insight into an effective approach for their classroom work.

Burton, E. J.,
Drama In Schools.
London: Jenkins, 1955.

Introduces the teacher to the value of dramatic work in education and suggests appropriate activities that can be used in specific grades from kindergarten through to secondary-school level.

Courtney, Richard,
Play, Drama and Thought.
London: Cassell, 1968.

An exhaustive and carefully annotated treatise on educational philosophy, psychology, sociology, and cognition, with particular emphasis on the educational use of drama and role-playing down through the ages.

Crosscup, Richard,
Children and Dramatics.
New York: Scribner's, 1966.

The author introduces the reader to the need of children for the broadening emotional experience of dramatics and outlines various ways in which an adult can use dramatics to contribute to a child's development.

Hartley, Ruth E., Lawrence K. Frank, and Robert M. Goldenson,
Understanding Children's Play.
New York and London: Columbia University Press, 1952.

Written by psychologists, the book presents records and case histories, especially of kindergarten classes, that explore the potentialities of play for a better understanding of young children.

McCaslim, Nellie,
Creative Drama In The Classroom.
New York: David McKay, 1968.

While each chapter in the book deals with a different aspect of Creative Dramatics in the classroom, all chapters converge on the simple purpose of providing a new dimension for learning that appeals to children and results in a positive response from them.

Siks, Geraldine Brain,
Creative Dramatics: An Art For Children.
New York: Harper and Row, 1958.

Written about the author's experiences in her extensive teaching of Creative Dramatics, the book contains many interesting accounts of children's responses to imaginative stimuli.

Slade, Peter,
Child Drama.
London: University of London Press, 1954.

A detailed analysis of Child Drama, its principles and its value in the education of children. The text is based on the author's penetrating observations of children's natural play patterns, upon which he evolves a method, defining its use for teachers, of helping the child realize his individual potentiality.

Slade, Peter,
An Introduction To Child Drama.
London: University of London Press, 1958.

A condensed version of the above volume with some additional suggestions on social drama.

Slade, Peter,
Experience In Spontaneity.
London: Longmans Green, 1968.

Partly autobiographical, this book is an historical account of the development of Child Drama, and it emphasizes Mr. Slade's method in youth and adult drama.

1000040696

WILKES COLLEGE LIBRARY